Praise for *Go in Peace*

"What might initially seem to be a conventional collection of devotions has at its heart a truly radical critique of most Western thought since the Enlightenment."

—PHILIP JENKINS, author of *The New Faces of Christianity*

"To read *Go in Peace* is like making a retreat with the pope as your spiritual director."

—FR. ANDREW GREELEY, author of
The Making of the Pope 2005

"Durepos has performed a valuable service by synthesizing the pope's thoughts in an easy-to-read format that inspires prayer and reflection."

—*Publishers Weekly*

"*Go in Peace* distills more than two decades of the teachings of John Paul II—the most important religious figure of the twentieth century."

—SCOTT HAHN, professor of Scripture and theology,
Franciscan University of Steubenville

"*Go in Peace* is the best and most readable one-volume introduction to the writings of Pope John Paul II."

—BERT GHEZZI, author of *Voices of the Saints*

"*Go in Peace* is a private audience with Pope John Paul II. . . . This volume fits the description it will soon earn: a spiritual classic for out time."

—EUGENE KENNEDY, author of *The Unhealed Wound*

Go in Peace

Go in Peace

A GIFT OF ENDURING LOVE

by

JOHN PAUL II

Edited by Joseph Durepos

LOYOLAPRESS.
CHICAGO

LOYOLAPRESS.

3441 N. ASHLAND AVENUE
CHICAGO, ILLINOIS 60657
(800) 621-1008
WWW.LOYOLABOOKS.ORG

The Scripture quotations contained herein are from the New Revised Standard Version Bible: Catholic Edition, copyright © 1993 and 1989 by the Division of Christian Education of the National Council of the Churches of Christ in the U.S.A. Used by permission. All rights reserved.

Go in Peace was selected, arranged, and edited by Joseph Durepos largely from materials originally published in *Celebrate the Third Millennium, Celebrate 2000,* and *The Prayers of Pope John Paul II,* edited by Paul Thigpen and published by Servant Publications, Inc.

All selections have been taken from the official Vatican translation of papal documents. Some are from encyclicals and apostolic letters published in the United States by Pauline Books & Media. Some texts appeared originally in *L'Osservatore Romano* (English edition, Via del Pellegrino, 00120 Vatican City, Europe), which is the official Vatican newspaper, and were reprinted in *The Pope Speaks (TPS),* a bimonthly periodical published by *Our Sunday Visitor* (200 Noll Plaza, Huntington, IN 46750). Used by permission. All rights reserved.

Cover photo: Corbis
Cover design: Judine O'Shea
Interior design: Eva Vincze

Library of Congress Cataloging-in-Publication Data

John Paul II, Pope, 1920–2005
 Go in peace : a gift of enduring love / by John Paul II ; edited by Joseph Durepos.
  p. cm.
 ISBN-10: 0-8294-1746-X   ISBN-13: 978-0-8294-1746-3
 1. Christian life—Catholic authors. 2. Catholic Church—Doctrines.
I. Durepos, Joseph, 1955– II. Title.
 BX2350.3 .J62 2003
 282—dc21

                                                      2002154072

First paperback printing, March 2007
paperback ISBN: 978-0-8294-2472-0

Printed in the United States of America
06 07 08 09 10 11 Versa 10 9 8 7 6 5 4 3 2 1

Peace is not a utopia, nor an inaccessible ideal,
nor an unrealizable dream. . . . Peace is possible.
—John Paul II

Lord, make me an instrument of your peace.
—St. Francis of Assisi

Lord Jesus Christ, you said to your apostles:
I leave you peace, my peace I give you.
—Rite of Peace
from the Mass

$\mathcal{C}$ontents

Introduction to the New Edition:
Images of John Paul II

When we think of Pope John Paul II, a variety of images, many of them quite personal, come into our minds.

My favorite mental picture of him is as a young, vigorous man in a dazzling white cassock emerging from the convention center in Philadelphia in 1979. I was there in the crowd that day, standing on the sidewalk with hundreds of other excited fans. As John Paul greeted the cheers, he turned his head and suddenly caught sight of a long line of young children confined to wheelchairs in front of the nearby Children's Hospital.

The new pope made his way to the children and spent nearly half an hour talking with them, embracing them, and blessing them. I can still see him, intently bending over their heads and gently touching each one of them as they looked up at him—with surprise and a little confusion. As I watched this, I wept—to my own surprise and a little confusion.

In 1979, I was a college student, and not a very religious one. Over the years, as my faith grew stronger and my relationship with the Church deepened, the figure of Pope John Paul II grew more distinct, like a slowly developing photo, taking on greater clarity in my life. I followed his exploits, as most Catholics did, and watched as the images changed: John Paul before throngs in Poland, John Paul with the poor in Africa, John Paul admonishing dictators, John Paul before the Western Wall in Jerusalem. Finally, I saw the bent and trembling John Paul, slowly dying before our sorrowful eyes as he labored through his final years of leading the Church.

Even as the images fade, we can begin to assess his enormous accomplishments. It is impossible in a few paragraphs to sum up the influence of Karol Wojtyła on the Church and the world. Any mere biographical sketch will mention a number of superlatives: the first-ever Polish pope, the first pope to visit a synagogue since the days of the early Church, the most widely traveled pope in history. Even the shortest biography will note how his astonishing involvement with the Solidarity movement in his native Poland helped pave the way for the dismantling of communism in Eastern Europe, then in the Soviet Union, and finally led to the end of the cold war. Any historical summary will point to his voluminous writings, most notably his powerful encyclicals on social justice, which challenge both socialist *and* capitalist systems to respect the essential dignity of every human person.

Assessments over, we are left with John Paul's words. And that's what you will find in this book: a collection of some of his most meaningful writings, arranged according to the themes he stressed again and again throughout his travels and in his many books, encyclicals, speeches, and letters.

This volume is a window into the marvelous humanity of Pope John Paul II, as well as into his obvious sanctity. As I read it, I was reminded of how arduous his long journey had been. He was a man whose faith was nurtured in the intensely pious atmosphere of early-twentieth-century Polish Catholicism, forged in the terrors of midcentury Nazi and communist regimes, and finally allowed to blossom fully, like a magnificent fruit tree, for the nourishment of the late-century world.

At the end of that journey, some reports said, John Paul's final word was "Amen," as if he had completed one great, long prayer—one that, like all human prayers, was imperfect and personal and incomplete, but always faithful to God.

For me, his most meaningful message wasn't even his own, though he repeated it often enough that many thought it had originated with him. "Be not afraid!" he would say, over and over, echoing the message that Jesus repeated insistently to his disciples and that bracketed his earthly life (at the Annunciation, Gabriel tells Mary not to fear; at the Resurrection, the risen Lord tells his disciples not to fear). When John Paul uttered those words, the world understood that they were hearing from a man who not only believed in fearlessness but also had experienced things that were truly fearful.

On the day that John Paul died, I felt myself back in Philadelphia all those years ago, as a young man standing under the bright sun alongside hundreds of people cheering for Pope John Paul II—cheering for his dedication, cheering for his faithfulness, cheering for his service, and cheering, most of all, for the man who would be a saint.

James Martin, SJ

Editor's Foreword to the New Edition

I immersed myself in the writings of Pope John Paul II for two reasons. First, like many millions of people, I was simply fascinated by the man. I was transfixed by his public persona. I was awestruck at his accomplishments. I wanted to study the words of one of the most influential public figures of our time.

The second reason was more personal. I delved into the writings of John Paul to find answers to questions that touched on my deepest convictions and hesitations: *What does it mean to be a Catholic and a Christian today? Why do we believe as we do?* Since I am a professional editor, and a compulsive reader, it made sense for me to seek answers in words. I certainly had many words to read. John Paul was perhaps the most prolific writer ever to be pope. His corpus includes fourteen encyclicals, forty-five apostolic letters, fifteen apostolic exhortations, eleven apostolic constitutions, hundreds of public addresses, numerous poems, five books, and a number of plays.

As I sifted through his words, I came to understand something surprising about John Paul. For

all his magnificent accomplishments—world states-
man, theologian, philosopher, Church leader—his
fundamental role is that of a humble pastor. He
knew something about how men and women can
find God. He understood how the power of God
can be released in our lives. His supreme desire was
that we come to embrace a faith that transforms
the way we work, the way we relate to other people,
and the way we live in the world.

This book is the work of my immersion in the
words of John Paul II. It contains what I believe to
be his most personal words—those that seem most
deeply felt, most compelling, and most clearly and
passionately stated. In the many millions of words
he wrote or spoke over the years of his papacy, I
looked for the heart of John Paul II—the ideas
that he seemed to communicate most urgently, and
those that I believe will be his legacy.

The arrangement of this material reflects John
Paul's priorities. The twelve chapters correspond
to themes that he returned to again and again in
all his writings and talks, including faith, prayer,
family, suffering, forgiveness, the Church, the
Eucharist, and, most passionately, Christ—Christ
as the answer to all life's mysteries. You will find
that John Paul II articulates an astonishingly
powerful vision of what it means to be a Christian

in our modern world. Through his words and ideas, you will also experience the compassion, the intellect, and the poetry of a great spiritual soul who has much to share with you about your journey to God.

I have framed each chapter with Scripture selections combined with John Paul's quotations and prayers. By doing so, I have tried to create a reading experience modeled on the great art of *lectio divina*, or sacred reading. The overall intent is for you to deepen your understanding of John Paul's mind and heart by allowing these words to penetrate your mind and heart.

My goal as editor of this collection was to provide a thematic presentation of John Paul's ideas, in his own words, through which the reader could navigate smoothly and easily. To present harmonious prose, I applied a style and occasionally adjusted syntax. Following the form used by John Paul II in his later Vatican-authorized publications, I have not cited the sources of scriptural quotations within the text. It was my intention to present the words of John Paul II without interruption, thus preserving his inspirational tone. For readers who would like to further explore the Bible quotations included in the text, a list of verses and their sources appears at the back of the book.

Many people helped me in this task. Special thanks go to George Lane, SJ, and Terry Locke of Loyola Press, who opened the door to this project and made many valuable comments; to my colleagues Matthew Diener and Jim Manney, who offered gracious and welcome editorial support all along the way; and to Paul Thigpen and Bert Ghezzi of Servant Publications. I am also indebted to my "circle of first readers": Carol Durepos, Cathy Danchisin, and Phyllis Tickle. I am especially grateful for the love and support of my wife, Betty, who always believes first.

Though the papacy of John Paul II has ended, his legacy lies tangibly before us in his writings. We can touch his books, hold his pages in our hands, take his words into our hearts. We should do this. He wanted us to. In so doing, we may discover that the secret to John Paul II's immense popularity was that he really believed in a faith that could change the world for the better. His words will bear eloquent witness to this hope for many years to come.

Joseph Durepos

Go in Peace

BY JOHN PAUL II

ONE

On Prayer

The breath of divine life . . . , *in its simplest and most common manner, expresses itself and makes itself felt in prayer.*

—John Paul II

Lord, teach us to pray.

—Luke 11:1

hen, on the slopes of the Mount of Olives, the apostles addressed Jesus with the words "Lord, teach us to pray," they were not asking an ordinary question; they were expressing one of the deepest needs of the human heart.

To tell the truth, today's world does not make much room for this need. The hectic pace of daily activity, combined with the noisy and often frivolous invasiveness of our means of communication, is certainly not conducive to the interior recollection required for prayer. Then, too, there is a

deeper difficulty: modern people have an increas-
ingly less religious view of the world and life. The
secularization process seems to have persuaded
them that the course of events can be sufficiently
explained by the interplay of this world's immanent
forces, independent of higher intervention.

What we need to foster, in ourselves and in
others, is a contemplative outlook. Such an outlook
arises from faith in the God of life, who has created
every individual as a wonder. It is the outlook of
those who see life in its deeper meaning, who grasp
its utter gratuitousness, its beauty, and its invitation to freedom and responsibility. It is the outlook
of those who do not presume to take possession of
reality, but instead accept it as a gift, discovering in
all things the reflection of the Creator and seeing
in every person their own living image.

Our difficult age has a special need for prayer. In
the course of history—both in the past and in the
present—many men and women have borne witness to the importance of prayer by consecrating
themselves to the praise of God and to the life of
prayer, especially in monasteries and convents. In
recent years, we have seen a growth in the number of people who, in ever more widespread move-
ments and groups, are giving first place to prayer

and seeking in prayer a renewal of their spiritual life. This is a significant and comforting sign, for from this experience there is coming a real contribution to the revival of prayer among the faithful, who have been helped to gain a clearer idea of the Holy Spirit as He who inspires in hearts a profound yearning for holiness.

In many individuals and many communities, there is a growing awareness that—even with all the rapid progress of technological and scientific civilization, and despite the real conquests and goals attained—humanity is threatened. In the face of this danger—and while, indeed, they are already experiencing the frightful reality of humanity's spiritual decadence—individuals and communities, guided by an inner sense of faith, are seeking the strength to raise humanity up again, to save us from ourselves, from our own errors and mistakes that often make harmful our very conquests. In this way, the times in which we are living are bringing the Holy Spirit closer to the many who are returning to prayer.

In some Christian circles, however, there is a widespread "functional" view of prayer that threatens to compromise its transcendent nature. Some claim that one can truly find God by being open to one's neighbor. Therefore, prayer would not mean being removed from the world's distractions in order to be recollected in conversation with God. It would rather be expressed in an unconditional commitment to charity for others. Authentic prayer, therefore, would be our works of charity alone.

In reality, however, because we are creatures—in and of ourselves incomplete and needy—we find ourselves spontaneously turning to Him who is the source of every gift, in order to praise Him, make intercession, and in Him seek to fulfill the tormenting desire which enflames our hearts. St. Augustine understood this quite well when he noted: "You have made us for yourself, O Lord, and our hearts are restless until they rest in you."

For this very reason, the experience of prayer as a basic act of the believer is common to all religions, including those in which there is only a rather vague belief in a personal God.

In the spiritual realm, no one lives for oneself alone. And salutary concern for the salvation of one's own soul is freed from fear and selfishness only when it becomes concern for the salvation of others as well. This is the reality of the communion of saints, of the mystery of "vicarious life," and of prayer as the means of union with Christ and His saints.

This outlook does not give into discouragement when confronted by those who are sick, suffering, outcast, or at death's door. Instead, in all these situations, it feels challenged to find meaning; and precisely in the face of every person, it finds a call to encounter, dialogue, and solidarity.

It is time for all of us to adopt this outlook, and to rediscover, with deep spiritual awe, the ability to revere and honor every person. Inspired by this contemplative outlook, we cannot but respond with songs of joy, praise, and thanksgiving for the priceless gift of life and for the mystery of every individual's call to share, through Christ, in the life of grace and in an existence of unending communion with God our Creator and Father.

Jesus urges us to "pray always without becoming weary." Christians know that for them prayer is as essential as breathing; and once they have tasted the sweetness of intimate conversation with God, they do not hesitate to immerse themselves in it with trusting abandonment.

The Holy Spirit—the breath of the divine life—in its simplest and most common manner expresses itself and makes itself felt in prayer. Wherever people are praying in the world, there the Holy Spirit is, the living breath of prayer.

The Holy Spirit is the gift that comes into our hearts together with prayer. In prayer He manifests Himself first of all and above all as the gift that "helps us in our weakness." This is the magnificent thought developed by St. Paul in the Letter to the Romans when he writes: "For we do not know how to pray as we ought, but that very Spirit intercedes with sighs too deep for words."

Therefore, the Holy Spirit not only enables us to pray, but guides us from within in prayer: he is present in our prayer and gives it a divine dimension. Thus, "God, who searches the heart, knows what is the mind of the Spirit, because the Spirit intercedes for the saints according to the will of God." Prayer, through the power of the Holy Spirit, becomes the ever more mature expression of the new human, who by means of this prayer participates in the divine life.

Prayer is also the revelation of the abyss that is the heart of man: a depth that comes from God and that only God can fill, precisely with the Holy Spirit. Prayer is the voice of all those who have no voice. Prayer makes us aware that everything—even evil—finds its principal and definitive reference point in God.

Prayer is not simply one occupation among many, but is at the center of our life in Christ. It turns our attention away from ourselves and directs it to the Lord. Prayer fills the mind with truth and gives hope to the heart. Without a deep experience of prayer, growth in the moral life will be shallow.

Our Father who art in heaven . . .

According to these words—Christ's answer to the apostle's request "teach us to pray"—everything is reduced to this single concept: to learn to pray means "to learn the Father." If we learn the Father in the full sense of the word, in its full dimension, we have learned everything.

To learn who the Father is means learning what absolute trust is. To learn the Father means acquiring the certainty that He does not refuse you even when everything—materially and psychologically—seems to indicate refusal. He never refuses you.

Prayer not only opens us up to a meeting with the Most High, but also disposes us to meeting with our neighbors, helping us to establish with everyone—without discrimination—relationships of respect, understanding, esteem, and love. Prayer is the bond that most effectively unites us all. It is through prayer that believers meet one another at a level where inequalities, misunderstandings, bitterness, and hostility are overcome; namely, before God. Prayer is the authentic expression of a right relationship with God and with others.

We need to reaffirm our need for intense, humble, confident, and persevering prayer, if the world is finally to become a dwelling place of peace.

Our relationship with God also demands times of explicit prayer in which the relationship becomes an intense dialogue involving every dimension of the person. "The Lord's Day" is the day of this relationship, when men and women raise their song to God and become the voice of all creation. This is precisely why it is also the day of rest. Speaking as it does of renewal and detachment, the interruption of the often-oppressive rhythm of work expresses the dependence of humanity and the cosmos upon God. The Lord's Day returns again and again to declare this principle within the weekly reckoning of time. The "Sabbath" has therefore been interpreted evocatively as a determining element in a kind of "sacred architecture" of time that marks biblical revelation. It recalls that the universe and history belong to God; and without a constant awareness of that truth, we cannot serve in the world as coworkers of the Creator.

All of us, through the different forms of spirituality by which we are inspired and that constitute the rich spiritual heritage of the Church and humanity, are trying to live truly Christian lives— as Christians "in the world" without being "of the world." For the lay faithful, this apostolic life calls for effective openness to our various environments in order to cause the evangelical "leaven" to penetrate them. It involves assuming multiple activities and responsibilities in all areas of human life: the family, professions, society, culture, and politics. It is by assuming these responsibilities competently and in deep union with God that you will fulfill your vocation as laity and Christians: you will sanctify yourselves and sanctify the world.

To remain united with God in the accomplishment of these tasks incumbent upon you is a vital necessity to bear witness to His love. Only a sacramental life and a life of prayer will enable this intimacy with the Lord to grow.

So, to take time to pray and to nourish prayer and activities through biblical, theological, and doctrinal study; and to live by Christ and His grace by receiving assiduously the sacraments of reconciliation and the Eucharist: such are the fundamental requirements of every deeply Christian life. Thus, the Holy Spirit will be the source both of our action and of our contemplation, which will then interpenetrate each other, support each other, and yield abundant fruit.

This deep unity between prayer and action is at the basis of all spiritual renewal. It is at the basis of the great enterprises of evangelization and construction of the world according to God's plan.

We hear within us, as a resounding echo, the words that Jesus spoke: "Apart from me you can do nothing." We feel not only the need, but even a categorical imperative, for great, intense, and growing prayer by all the faithful. Only prayer can prevent all our great succeeding tasks and difficulties from becoming a source of crisis, and make them instead the occasion and, as it were, the foundation for ever more mature achievements on the People of God's march towards the Promised Land in this stage of history at the beginning of the third millennium.

Accordingly, and with a warm and humble call, I wish the Church and all its people to devote themselves in prayer—together with Mary the Mother of Jesus—as the apostles and disciples of the Lord did in the Upper Room in Jerusalem after Christ's ascension. Above all, I implore Mary, the heavenly Mother of the Church, to be so good as to devote herself to a prayer for humanity's new advent, together with us who make up the Church, that is to say the Mystical Body of her only Son. I hope that through this prayer we shall all be able to receive the Holy Spirit coming upon us, and thus become Christ's witnesses "to the ends of the earth," like those who went forth from Jerusalem on the day of Pentecost.

Likewise the Spirit helps us in our weakness; for we do not know how to pray as we ought, but that very Spirit intercedes with sighs too deep for words. And God, who searches the heart, knows what is the mind of the Spirit, because the Spirit intercedes for the saints according to the will of God.

—ROMANS 8:26–27

LISTEN TO US, O LORD!
In the spirit of Christ, our Lord, let us pray for
the Catholic Church,
for the other Churches, for the whole of mankind.
Listen to us, O Lord!
Let us pray for all those who suffer persecution
for the sake of justice
and for those who are striving for freedom
and peace.
Listen to us, O Lord!
Let us pray for those who exercise a ministry in
the Church,
for those who have special responsibilities in
social life,
and for all those who are in the service of the
little and the weak.
Listen to us, O Lord!
Let us ask God for the courage to persevere
in our commitment for the realization of the
unity of all Christians.
Listen to us, O Lord!
Lord God, we trust in You. Grant that we may
act in a way that is pleasing to You.
Grant that we may be faithful servants of
Your glory.
Amen.

—JOHN PAUL II

TWO

On Forgiveness
and Reconciliation

Forgiveness, in its truest and highest form, is a free act of love. But precisely because it is an act of love, it has its own intrinsic demands: the first of which is respect for the truth.

—JOHN PAUL II

୬ৡ৩

If we say that we have no sin, we deceive ourselves, and the truth is not in us. If we confess our sins, he who is faithful and just will forgive us our sins and cleanse us from all unrighteousness.

—1 JOHN 1:8–9

*M*ore than anyone else, the Christian ought to feel the obligation to conform their conscience to the truth. Before the splendor of the free gift of God's revelation in Christ, how humbly and attentively must we listen to the voice of conscience. How modest must we be in regard to our own limited insight. How quick must we be to learn and how slow to condemn. One of the constant temptations in every age, even among Christians, is to make oneself the norm of truth. In an age of pervasive individualism, this temptation takes a variety of forms, but the mark of those who are in the truth is the ability to love humbly. This is what Jesus teaches us: truth is expressed in love.

It is also Jesus who, especially in the parable of the Prodigal Son, makes us understand that sin is an offense against the love of the Father. The great gift that Jesus gives us in this parable is the comforting and reassuring revelation of the merciful love of a Father who, with his arms open wide, awaits the Prodigal Son's return, hurrying to embrace and pardon him, canceling all the consequences of sin, and celebrating the feast of new life for him.

From the first centuries, the Church has always been profoundly convinced that pardon, freely granted by God, implies a real change of life, the gradual elimination of evil within, and a renewal in our way of living. This sacramental action has to be combined with an existential act, with a real cleansing from fault, precisely what is called "penance." Pardon does not imply that this existential process becomes superfluous, but rather that it acquires a meaning that is accepted and welcomed.

The sacrament of penance offers the sinner a new possibility to convert and to recover the grace of justification won by the sacrifice of Christ. The sinner thus enters the life of God anew and shares fully in the life of the Church. Confessing his own sins, the believer truly receives pardon and can once more take part in the Eucharist as the sign that he has again found communion with the Father.

In the sacrament of penance—the sacrament of confession and reconciliation—every soul relives as its personal history the Gospel account of the tax collector, who left the temple justified: "But the tax collector, standing far off, would not even look up to heaven, but was beating his breast and saying, 'God, be merciful to me, a sinner!' I tell you, this man went down to his home justified rather than the other; for all who exalt themselves will be humbled, but all who humble themselves will be exalted."

To acknowledge one's misery in the sight of God is not to abase oneself, but to live the truth of one's own condition, and thus to obtain the true greatness of justice and grace after falling into sin. It is, in fact, to rise to the loftiest peace of spirit, by rising into a living relationship with God, who is merciful and faithful. The truth thus lived is the only thing in the human condition that makes us free.

Sin's essential nature is that of an offense against God. It is an offense against the divine majesty. We must also say that it is an act that offends the divine charity in that it is an infraction of the law of friendship and the covenant that God has established for His people. Therefore, it is an act of infidelity and, in practice, a rejection of His love.

Sin, therefore, is not a simple human error, nor does it cause damage only to the person. It is an offense against God in that the sinner disobeys the law of the Creator and Lord, and thus offends His paternal love. Sin draws its significance from the person's relationship to God.

As a rupture with God, sin is an act of disobedience by creatures who reject, at least implicitly, the very One from whom they came and who sustains them in life. It is therefore a suicidal act. Since by sinning people refuse to submit to God, their internal balance is destroyed, and it is precisely within themselves that contradictions and conflicts arise.

Wounded in this way, humans almost inevitably cause damage to the fabric of their relationships with others and with the created world. This is an objective law and an objective reality, verified in so many ways in the human psyche and in the spiritual life, as well as in society, where it is easy to see the signs and effects of internal disorder.

The mystery of sin is composed of this twofold wound that sinners open in themselves and in their relationships with their neighbors. Therefore, one can speak of personal and social sin: from one point of view, every sin is personal; from another point of view, every sin is social because it has social repercussions.

Sin, in the proper sense, is always a personal act since it is an act of freedom on the part of an individual person, and not properly of a group or community. This individual may be conditioned, incited, and influenced by numerous and powerful external factors. He may also be subjected to tendencies, defects, and habits linked with his personal condition. In many cases, such external and internal factors may attenuate, to a greater or lesser degree, the person's freedom, and therefore his responsibility and guilt.

But it is by the truth of faith, also confirmed by our experience and reason, that the human person is free. This truth cannot be disregarded in order to place the blame for an individual's sins on external factors such as structures, systems, or other people. Above all, this would be to deny the person's dignity and freedom, which are manifested—even though in a negative and disastrous way—in his responsibility for the sin committed. There is nothing so personal and nontransferable in each individual as merit for virtue or responsibility for sin.

Like all things human, the conscience can fail and encounter illusions and errors. It is a delicate voice that can be overpowered by a noisy, distracted way of life, or almost suffocated by a long-lasting and serious habit of sin.

Conscience needs to be nurtured and educated, and the preferred way to form it—at least for those who have the grace of faith—is to relate it to the biblical revelation of the moral law, authoritatively interpreted with the help of the Church and the Holy Spirit.

Throughout His life, Jesus proclaimed God's forgiveness, but He also taught the need for mutual forgiveness as the condition for obtaining it. In the Lord's Prayer, He makes us pray: "Forgive us our trespasses, as we forgive those who trespass against us." With that *as*, He places in our hands the measure with which we shall be judged by God.

The parable of the unforgiving servant, punished for his hardness of heart toward his fellow servant, teaches us that those who are unwilling to forgive exclude themselves from divine forgiveness by this very fact: "So my heavenly Father will also do to every one of you, if you do not forgive your brother or sister from your heart."

Our prayer itself cannot be pleasing to the Lord unless it is preceded, and in a certain sense "guaranteed" in its authenticity, by a sincere effort on our part to be reconciled with our brother and sister who may have "something against us"; only then will it be possible for us to present an offering pleasing to God.

The difficulty of forgiving does not arise only from circumstances of the present. History carries with it a heavy burden of violence and conflict that cannot easily be shed. Abuses of power, oppression, and wars have brought suffering to countless human beings; and even if the causes of these sad events are lost in the distant past, their destructive effects live on, fueling fear, suspicion, hatred, and division among families, ethnic groups, and whole peoples. These are facts that sorely try the goodwill of those who are seeking to overcome their past conditioning.

The truth is that one cannot remain a prisoner of the past, for individuals and peoples need a sort of "healing of memories" so that past evils will not come back again. This does not mean forgetting past events; it means reexamining them with a new attitude and learning precisely from the experience of suffering that only love can produce healing, whereas hatred produces only devastation and ruin.

Certainly, forgiveness does not come spontaneously or naturally to people. Forgiving from the heart can sometimes be heroic—the pain of losing a child, a brother or sister, one's parents, or one's whole family as a result of war, terrorism, or criminal acts can lead to the total closing off of oneself from others. People who have been left with nothing because they have been deprived of their land and home, refugees, and those who have endured the humiliation of violence cannot fail to feel the temptation for hatred and revenge. Only the warmth of human relationships marked by respect, understanding, and acceptance can help them to overcome such feelings. Thanks to the healing power of love, even the most wounded heart can experience the liberating encounter with forgiveness.

Real peace is not just a matter of structures and mechanisms. It rests, above all, on the adoption of a style of human coexistence marked by mutual acceptance and a capacity to forgive from the heart. We all need to be forgiven by others, so we must all be ready to forgive. Asking and granting forgiveness is something profoundly worthy of every one of us; sometimes it is the only way out of situations marked by age-old and violent hatred.

Forgiveness, in its truest and highest form, is a free act of love; but precisely because it is an act of love, it has its own intrinsic demands: the first of which is respect for the truth.

God alone is absolute truth, but He made the human heart open to the desire for truth, which He then fully revealed in His Incarnate Son. Hence, we are all called to live the truth. Forgiveness, far from precluding the search for truth, actually requires it. Evil that has been done must be acknowledged and, as far as possible, corrected.

Another essential prerequisite for forgiveness and reconciliation is justice, which finds its ultimate foundation in the law of God and in His plan of love and mercy for humanity. Understood in this way, justice is not limited to establishing what is right between the parties in conflict, but looks, above all, to reestablishing authentic relationships with God, with oneself, and with others. Thus, there is no contradiction between forgiveness and justice. Forgiveness neither eliminates nor lessens the need for the reparation that justice requires, but seeks to reintegrate individuals and groups into society, and countries into the community of nations. No punishment should suppress the inalienable dignity of those who have committed evil. The door to repentance and rehabilitation must always remain open.

We must learn to read the history of other peoples without facile and partisan bias, making an effort to understand their point of view. This is a real challenge at the level of education and culture. This is a very real challenge for civilization. If we agree to set out on this journey, we shall come to see that mistakes are not all on one side. We shall see how history has sometimes been presented in a distorted and even manipulated way, with tragic results.

A correct reading of history will make it easier to accept and appreciate the social, cultural, and religious differences between individuals and groups. This is the first step toward reconciliation, since respect for differences is an inherently necessary condition for genuine relationships between individuals and between groups. The suppression of differences can result in apparent peace, but it creates a volatile situation that is, in fact, the prelude to fresh outbreaks of violence.

We must ask ourselves: Can we be fully reconciled with Christ without being fully reconciled among ourselves? Can we bear joint and effective witness to Christ if we are not reconciled with one another? Can we be reconciled with one another without forgiving one another? Forgiveness is the condition for reconciliation, but this cannot take place without interior transformation and conversion—which is the work of grace.

With deep conviction, I wish to appeal to everyone to seek peace along the paths of forgiveness. I am fully aware that forgiveness can seem contrary to human logic, which often yields to the dynamics of conflict and revenge; but forgiveness is inspired by the logic of love, the love that God has for every man and woman, for every people and nation, and for the whole human family.

Jesus bent down and wrote with his finger on the ground. When they kept on questioning him, he straightened up and said to them, "Let anyone among you who is without sin be the first to throw a stone at her." And once again he bent down and wrote on the ground. When they heard it, they went away, one by one, beginning with the elders; and Jesus was left alone with the woman standing before him. Jesus straightened up and said to her, "Woman, where are they? Has no one condemned you?" She said, "No one, sir." And Jesus said, "Neither do I condemn you. Go your way, and from now on do not sin again."

—John 8:6–11

To the People of Our Time,
so sensitive to the proof of concrete living
witness,
the Church is called upon to give an example of
reconciliation,
particularly within herself.
And for this purpose let us work to bring peace
to people's minds,
to reduce tensions, to overcome divisions, and to
heal wounds
that may have been inflicted by one upon another.
We must try to be united in what is essential for
Christian faith and life,
in accordance with the ancient maxim:
"In what is doubtful, freedom; in what is
necessary, unity; in all things, charity."
Unity must be the result of a true conversion
of everyone,
the result of mutual forgiveness,
of prayer and of complete docility to the action of
the Holy Spirit,
who is the Spirit of reconciliation.
Amen.

—John Paul II

THREE

On Jesus

Jesus Christ is the new beginning of everything. In Him all things come into their own; they are taken up and given back to the Creator from whom they first came. Christ is thus the fulfillment of the yearning of all the world's religions and, as such, He is their sole and definitive completion.

—JOHN PAUL II

Jesus said to him, "I am the way, and the truth, and the life. No one comes to the Father except through me."

—JOHN 14:6

THE BEATITUDES

Blessed are the poor in spirit, for theirs is the
kingdom of heaven.
Blessed are those who mourn, for they will
be comforted.
Blessed are the meek, for they will inherit
the earth.
Blessed are those who hunger and thirst for
righteousness, for they will be filled.
Blessed are the merciful, for they will receive
mercy.
Blessed are the pure in heart, for they will
see God.
Blessed are the peacemakers, for they will be
called children of God.
Blessed are those who are persecuted for
righteousness' sake, for theirs is the kingdom
of heaven.
Blessed are you when people revile you and
persecute you and utter all kinds of evil against
you falsely on my account. Rejoice and be glad,
for your reward is great in heaven, for in the
same way they persecuted the prophets who
were before you.

—MATTHEW 5:3-12

The mystery of the Incarnation has given a tremendous impetus to humanity's thought and artistic genius. Precisely by reflecting upon the union of two natures, human and divine, in the Person of the Incarnate Word, Christian thinkers have come to explain the concept of person as the unique and unrepeatable center of freedom and responsibility, whose inalienable dignity must be realized. This concept of the person has proved to be the cornerstone of a genuinely human civilization.

Also, the great ideal of the Beatitudes remains for humanity—for men and women of every time, every place, and every culture—an incomparable source of inspiration by the wonder it arouses and by the way it expands our capacity to be and to act, to contemplate and to create.

Faith in Christ, the Incarnate Word, leads us to see humanity in a new light. It enables us to believe in humanity, created in the image and likeness of God, at once a microcosm of the world and an icon of God. The resurrection of Jesus is the fundamental event upon which Christian faith rests. It is an astonishing reality, fully grasped in the light of faith, yet historically attested to by those who were privileged to see the Risen Lord. It is a wondrous event that is not only absolutely unique in human history, but lies at the very heart of the mystery of time.

In the incarnation of the Son of God, we see forged the enduring and definitive synthesis that the human mind itself could not even have imagined: the Eternal enters time; the Whole lies hidden in the part; God takes on a human face. The truth communicated in Christ's revelation is therefore no longer confined to a particular place or culture, but is offered to every man and woman who would welcome it as the Word that is the absolutely valid source of meaning for human life.

Now, in Christ, all have access to the Father, since by His death and resurrection Christ has bestowed on humanity the divine life that the first Adam refused. Through this revelation, men and women are offered the ultimate truth about their own lives and about the goal of history. Seen in any other terms, the mystery of personal existence remains an insoluble riddle. Where might human beings seek the answer to dramatic questions such as pain, the suffering of the innocent, and death, if not from the mystery of Christ's passion, death, and resurrection?

Jesus does not merely speak in the name of God like the Prophets, but He is God Himself speaking through His Eternal Word Made Flesh. Here we touch upon the essential point by which Christianity differs from all other religions, by which humanity's search for God has been expressed from earliest times: Christianity has its starting point in the Incarnation of the Word.

Here, it is not simply a case of a people seeking God, but of God who comes in Person to speak to us of Himself and to show us the path by which He may be reached. This is what is proclaimed in John's Gospel: "No one has ever seen God. It is God the only Son, who is close to the Father's heart, who has made him known." The Incarnate Word is thus the fulfillment of the yearning present in all the religions of humanity: this fulfillment is brought about by God Himself and transcends all human expectations. It is the mystery of grace.

In Jesus Christ, God not only speaks to us, but also seeks us out. The Incarnation of the Son of God attests that God goes in search of each of us. Jesus speaks of this search as the Shepherd seeking his lost sheep.

It is a search that begins in the heart of God and culminates in the Incarnation of the Word. If God goes in search of each of us, created in His own image and likeness, He does so because He loves us eternally in the Word and wishes to raise us in Christ to the dignity of adoptive sons and daughters. God therefore goes in search of us all, who are His special possessions in a way unlike any other creature. We are God's possession by virtue of a choice made in love: God seeks us out, moved by His fatherly heart.

Why does God seek us out? Because we have turned away from Him, hiding ourselves as Adam and Eve did among the trees of the Garden of Eden. We've allowed ourselves to be led astray by the enemy of God. Satan deceived humanity, persuading us that we were as God, that we, like God, were capable of knowing good and evil, ruling the world according to our own will without having to take into account the divine will.

Going in search of humanity through His Son, God wishes to persuade us to abandon the paths of evil, which lead us farther and farther afield. Making us abandon those paths means making us understand that we are taking the wrong path; it means overcoming the evil that is everywhere found in our human history. Overcoming evil: this is the meaning of the Redemption.

This is brought about in the sacrifice of Christ, by which humanity redeems the debt of sin and is reconciled to God. The Son of God became a person, taking a body and soul in the womb of the Virgin, precisely for this reason: to become the perfect redeeming sacrifice. The religion of the Incarnation is the religion of the world's Redemption through the sacrifice of Christ, wherein lies victory over evil, over sin, and over death itself. Accepting death on the Cross, Christ at the same time reveals and gives life because He rises again and death no longer has power over Him.

Jesus meets the men and women of every age, including our own, with the same words: "You will know the truth, and the truth will make you free." These words contain both a fundamental requirement and a warning: the requirement of an honest relationship with regard to truth as a condition for authentic freedom, and the warning to avoid every kind of illusory freedom, every freedom that fails to enter into the whole truth about our lives and the world.

Today, even after two thousand years, we see Christ as the One who brings humanity freedom based on truth—freeing men and women from what curtails, diminishes, and breaks off this freedom at its root, in our souls, our hearts, and our consciences.

Jesus came to provide the ultimate answer to the yearning for life and for the infinite that His heavenly Father had poured into our hearts when He created us. At the culmination of this revelation, the Incarnate Word, Jesus Christ, proclaims, "I am the life" and "I came that they may have life."

On Jesus 45

But what life? Jesus' intention was clear: the very life of God, which surpasses all the possible aspirations of the human heart.

Our daily experience tells us that life is marked by sin and threatened by death, despite the desire for good that beats in our hearts and the desire for life that courses through our veins. Whatever little heed we pay to ourselves and to the frustrations that life brings us, we discover that everything within us impels us to transcend ourselves, urges us to overcome the temptation of superficiality or despair. It is then that human beings are called to become disciples of the One who infinitely transcends them, in order to enter at last into true life.

Left to ourselves, we could never achieve the ends for which we have been created. Within us there is a promise that we find we are incapable of attaining. But the Son of God who came among us has given us His personal assurance: "I am the way, and the truth, and the life." As St. Augustine so strikingly phrased it, Christ "wishes to create a place in which it is possible for all people to find true life." This "place" is His Body and His Spirit, in which the whole of human life, redeemed and forgiven, is renewed and made divine.

What does Christ ask of you? Jesus asks you not to be ashamed of Him and to commit yourself to proclaiming Him to your peers. Do not be afraid because Jesus is with you. Do not be afraid of getting lost: the more you give of yourself, the more you will find yourself.

Jesus is the Way, the Truth, and the Life. The way of Christ is the virtuous, fruitful, and peaceful life as children of God and as brothers and sisters in the same human family. The truth of Christ is the eternal truth of God, who has revealed Himself to us not only in the created world, but also through Sacred Scripture, and especially in and through His Son, Jesus Christ, the Word made flesh. And the life of Christ is the life of grace, that free gift of God, which is a created share in His own life and which enables us to live forever in His love.

When Christians are truly convinced of this, their lives are transformed. This transformation results not only in a credible and compelling witness, but also in an urgent and effective communication, of a living faith that paradoxically increases as it is shared.

Know Jesus. Be the first to know Him: through constant reading and meditation; through prayer that is an ongoing dialogue between life and the Word of God.

Know the gospel. Know the gospel by seeking help from wise guides and witnesses to Christ. Ask for help to know and live that love which is the heart of the gospel. By knowing the gospel, you will encounter Christ—and do not be afraid of what He may ask of you. Because Christ is demanding, thank God. He is demanding. If He were not demanding, there would be nothing to listen to, nothing to follow.

Now more than ever, in a world that is often without light and without the courage of noble ideals, people need the fresh, vital spirituality of the gospel. Do not be afraid to go out on the streets and into public places, like the first apostles who preached Christ and the good news of salvation in the squares of cities, towns, and villages. This is no time to be ashamed of the gospel. It is the time to preach it from the rooftops. Do not be afraid to break out of comfortable and routine modes of living in order to take up the challenge of making Christ known in the modern metropolis. It is you who must "go out into the roads and lanes" and invite everyone you meet to the banquet that God has prepared for His people.

The gospel must not be kept hidden because of fear or indifference. It was not meant to be hidden away in private. It has to be put on a stand so that people may see its light and give praise to our heavenly Father.

Jesus went in search of the men and women of His time. He engaged them in an open and truthful dialogue, whatever their condition. As the Good Samaritan of the human family, He became close to people, close enough to heal them of their sins and of the wounds that life inflicted upon them, and brought them back into the Father's house.

There are times and circumstances when it is necessary to make decisive choices in our lives. When we are experiencing difficult times, it can be hard to distinguish good from evil, true teachers from false teachers. Jesus warned us: "Beware that no one leads you astray. For many will come in my name, saying, 'I am the Messiah!'" and "My time is near." Do not be misled by these false teachers.

Instead, pray and listen to Jesus' words. Let yourself be guided by His truth. Do not succumb to the world's flattery and facile illusions, which frequently become tragic disappointments. There are no shortcuts to happiness and light.

Above all, seek Jesus. Let your life be a continual, sincere search for the Savior, without ever tiring, without ever abandoning the undertaking; even though darkness shall fall upon your spirit, temptations beset you, and grief and incomprehension wring your heart. These are things that are a part of life here below; they are inevitable, but they can also do good because they mature our spirit. You must never turn back, however, even if it should seem to you that the light of Christ is fading. On the contrary, continue to seek with renewed faith and greater generosity.

Try to discover where He is, and you will be able to gather from everyone some detail that will indicate it to you, that will tell you where He lives. Ask souls that are meek, repentant, generous, humble, and hidden; ask your brothers and sisters, far and near, because you will find in everyone something that indicates Jesus to you. Ask, above all, your soul and your conscience, because they will be able to indicate to you, in an unmistakable way, a mark of His passing, a trace of His power and His love.

But ask humbly. That is, let your soul be ready to see, outside itself, those parts of His goodness that God has sown in creatures. To seek Him every day means possessing Him a little more every day, being admitted a little at a time to an intimacy with Him; and then you will be able to understand better the sound of His voice, the meaning of His language, the reason for His coming to earth and for His sacrifice on the Cross.

Let the same mind be in you that was in Christ Jesus,
   who, though he was in the form of God,
   did not regard equality with God
   as something to be exploited,
but emptied himself,
   taking the form of a slave,
   being born in human likeness.
And being found in human form,
   he humbled himself
   and became obedient to the point of death—
   even death on a cross.

Therefore God also highly exalted him
   and gave him the name
   that is above every name,
so that at the name of Jesus
   every knee should bend,
   in heaven and on earth and under the earth,
and every tongue should confess
   that Jesus Christ is Lord,
   to the glory of God the Father.

                —PHILIPPIANS 2:5–11

The Majesty of Christ the Teacher

and the unique consistency and persuasiveness of
   His teaching,
His words, His parables, and His arguments,
which are never separable from His life and His
   very being.
His silences, His miracles, His gestures, His
   prayer, His love for people,
His special affection for the little and the poor,
His acceptance of the total sacrifice on the Cross
   for the redemption of the world,
and His resurrection are the actualization of
His Word and the fulfillment of revelation.
For Christians the crucifix is one of the most
   sublime and
popular images of Christ the Teacher.
The Teacher who reveals God to man and man
   to himself,
the Teacher who saves, sanctifies, and guides,
who lives, who speaks, rouses, moves, redresses,
   judges, forgives,
and goes with us day by day on the path of history,
and the Teacher who will come again in glory.
Amen.

            —John Paul II

FOUR

On Faith and Belief

Whether we admit it or not, there comes for everyone the moment when personal existence must be anchored to a truth recognized as final, a truth that confers a certitude no longer open to doubt.

—JOHN PAUL II

❦

Do you not believe that I am in the Father and the Father is in me? The words that I say to you I do not speak on my own; but the Father who dwells in me does his works. Believe me that I am in the Father and the Father is in me; but if you do not, then believe me because of the works themselves. . . .

I will do whatever you ask in my name, so that the Father may be glorified in the Son. If in my name you ask me for anything, I will do it.

—JOHN 14:10–11, 13–14

here are in the lives of human beings many more truths that are simply believed than truths that are acquired by way of personal verification. Who, for instance, could assess critically the countless scientific findings upon which modern life is based? Who could personally examine the flow of information that comes day after day from all parts of the world and that is generally accepted as true? Who in the end could forge anew the paths of experience and thought that have yielded the treasures of human wisdom and religion? This means that the human being—the one who seeks truth—is also the one who lives by belief.

In believing, we trust ourselves to the knowledge acquired by other people. This suggests an important tension. On the one hand, the knowledge acquired through belief can seem an imperfect form of knowledge, to be perfected gradually through personal accumulation of evidence. On the other hand, belief is often humanly richer than mere evidence because it involves an interpersonal relationship and brings into play not only a person's capacity to know, but also the deeper capacity to entrust oneself to others, to enter into a relationship with another, which is intimate and enduring.

Most people eventually seek an absolute, something to give all their searching a meaning and an answer—something ultimate, which might serve as the ground of all things. In other words, they seek a final explanation, a supreme value, something that puts an end to all their questioning. Whether we admit it or not, there comes for everyone the moment when personal existence must be anchored to a truth recognized as final, a truth that confers a certitude no longer open to doubt.

In Jesus, religion is no longer a blind search for God. It is a response of faith to a God who reveals Himself. It is a response in which humanity speaks to God as our Creator and Father, a response made possible by the one Man in whom God speaks to each individual person and by whom each individual person is enabled to respond to God.

What is more, in this Man all creation responds to God. Jesus Christ is the new beginning of everything. In Him all things come into their own, they are taken up and given back to the Creator from whom they first came. Christ is thus the fulfillment of the yearning of all the world's religions and, as such, He is their sole and definitive completion.

Just as God in Christ speaks to humanity of Himself, so in Christ all of humanity and the whole of creation speaks of itself to God—indeed, it gives itself to God.

To believe, to have faith, means accepting the truth that comes from God with the whole conviction of the intellect, relying on the grace of the

Holy Spirit—"whom God has given to those who obey him"—accepting what God has revealed and what always reaches us by means of the Church in her living transmission, that is, in tradition. The channel of this tradition is the teaching of Peter and the apostles and their successors.

To believe means accepting their witness in the Church, which guards this witness from generation to generation, and then—on the basis of this witness—to bear witness to the same truth, with the same certainty and interior conviction.

What is our faith? Is our faith as univocal and clear as the faith confessed by Peter before the Sanhedrin? Or is it not, on the contrary, sometimes ambiguous? Mingled with suspicions and doubts? Mutilated? Adapted to our human points of view? To the criteria of fashion, feeling, human opinion? Can we really make Peter's words our own: "We must obey God rather than any human authority"?

Over the course of centuries, the "Sanhedrins" that demand silence, abandonment, or distortion of this truth change. These Sanhedrins of our modern world are different than St. Peter's—and they are numerous. They are the individual men and women who reject divine truth; they are the systems of human thought, of human knowledge; they are the different conceptions of the world, and also the different programs of human behavior. They are also the various forms of pressure from so-called public opinion, of mass civilization, and of the media with its social communications of a materialistic, agnostic, and antireligious hue. They are, finally, some of the contemporary systems of government that—if they do not deprive citizens completely of the possibility of confessing the faith—at least limit it in various ways, exclude believers, and make them second-class citizens.

Before all these modern forms of the Sanhedrin of Peter's time, the answer of faith must always remain the same: "We must obey God rather than any human authority."

The apostles asked of Jesus: "Increase our faith!" This too must be our constant prayer. Faith is always demanding because faith leads us beyond ourselves. It leads us directly to God. Faith also imparts a vision of life's purpose and stimulates us to action. The gospel of Jesus Christ is not a private opinion, a remote spiritual ideal, or a mere program for personal growth. The gospel is the power that can transform the world.

This gospel is no abstraction: it is the living Person of Jesus Christ, the Word of God, the reflection of the Father's glory, the Incarnate Son who reveals the deepest meaning of our humanity and the noble destiny to which the whole human family is called. Christ has commanded us to let the light of the gospel shine forth in our service to society. How can we profess faith in God's Word, and then refuse to let it inspire and direct our thinking, our activity, our decisions, and our responsibilities toward one another?

Who, in fact, is the Christian? A person whom "Christ Jesus has made . . . his own," and who therefore longs to make Him known and loved everywhere, "to the ends of the earth." Our faith spurs us to be His witnesses. If this does not occur, it means that our faith is still incomplete, partial, and immature.

Remember: just as the Spirit transformed the first band of disciples into courageous apostles of the Lord and enlightened preachers of His Word, He continues to prepare witnesses for the gospel in our times.

It is essential that we rediscover and set forth once more the authentic reality of our Christian faith, which is not simply a set of propositions to be accepted with intellectual assent. Rather, faith is the lived knowledge of Christ, a living remembrance of His commandments, and a truth to be lived out. Faith is a decision involving one's whole existence. It is an encounter, a dialogue, a communion of love and of life between the believer and Jesus Christ, the Way, the Truth, and the Life. It entails an act of trusting abandonment to Christ, which enables us to live as He lived, in profound love of God and of our brothers and sisters.

Faith also possesses a moral content. It gives rise to and calls for a consistent life commitment; it entails and brings to perfection the acceptance and observance of God's commandments. As St. John writes: "Now by this we may be sure that we know him, if we obey his commandments."

Through the moral life, faith becomes "confession," not only before God, but also before humanity; it becomes witness. "You are the light of the world," said Jesus. "Let your light shine before others, so that they may see your good works and give glory to your Father in heaven."

We must be firm in our faith. Be so in the first place by means of thorough and gradual knowledge of the content of Christian doctrines. It is not enough to be Christians because of the Baptism received or because of the historical and social conditions in which we are born and live. As we grow in years and culture, new problems and new requirements of clarity come into consciousness. It is then necessary to set out in a responsible way in search of the motivations of our own Christian faith.

Make time for study, meditation, and reflection. Use your intelligence well; make an effort to reach correct convictions; do not waste time; deepen the motives and foundations of faith in Christ and in the Church, so as to be firm now and in your future. We remain firm in our faith by means of prayer; remember St. Paul wrote: "Pray without ceasing."

Be wise, for it is possible to know Holy Scripture perfectly, to be learned in philosophy and theology, and yet not have faith, or fail in faith, because it is always God who calls first to know Him and love Him in the right way.

It is necessary, therefore, to be humble before the Almighty. It is necessary to maintain the sense of mystery because there always remains the infinite between God and man. It is necessary to remember that, before God and His Revelation, it is not so much a question of understanding with one's own limited reason, but rather of loving.

If we are truly open to the action of the Spirit, we will succeed in reflecting and radiating to others the mystery of love that dwells within us. We are its witnesses. Witnesses of shining, integral faith; of active, patient, and kindly charity; of service for the many forms of poverty experienced by contemporary humanity. Witnesses of the hope that does not disappoint and of the deep communion that reflects the life of God; of obedience; and of the Cross. In short, witnesses of holiness, "people of the Beatitudes." We are called to be perfect, as the heavenly Father is perfect.

May our faith be certain, that is, founded on the Word of God, on deep knowledge of the Gospel message, and especially of the life, person, and work of Christ, and also on the interior witness of the Holy Spirit.

May our faith be strong; may it not hesitate, nor waver, before the doubts, the uncertainties

that philosophical systems or fashionable move-
ments would like to suggest to us; may it not
descend to compromises with certain concepts
that would like to present Christianity as a mere
ideology at the same level as so many others, now
outdated.

May our faith be joyful because it is based on
awareness of possessing a divine gift; and when we
pray, when we speak with God, and when we con-
verse with others, let us manifest the joy of this
enviable possession.

Finally, let our faith be active, let it manifest itself
and take on concrete shape in our labors and our
generous charity toward our brothers and sisters,
some of whom live crushed in sorrow and in need;
let our faith be manifested in our serene adherence to the teaching of the truth; let our faith be
expressed in our availability for all apostolic initia-
tives in which we are called upon to participate for
the expansion and the building up of the Kingdom
of God.

Our faith, our belief, are like two wings on
which the human spirit rises to the contemplation
of truth; and God has placed in the human heart
this desire to know the truth—in a word, to know

Himself—so that, by knowing and loving God, men and women may also come to know the fullness of the truth about themselves.

I have been crucified with Christ; and it is no longer I who live, but it is Christ who lives in me. And the life I now live in the flesh I live by faith in the Son of God, who loved me and gave himself for me.

—GALATIANS 2:19–20

**FAITH TEACHES US THAT MAN'S DESTINY IS
WRITTEN IN THE HEART AND MIND OF GOD,**
who directs the course of history.
It also teaches us that the Father puts in our
  hands the task
of beginning to build here on earth the kingdom
  of heaven,
which the Son came to announce
and which will find its fulfillment at the end
  of time.
It is our duty, then, to live in history, side by side
  with our peers,
sharing their worries and hopes because
  Christians are
and must be fully people of their time.
We cannot escape into another dimension,
  ignoring the tragedies of our era,
closing our eyes and hearts to the anguish that
  pervades life.
On the contrary, it is we who, though not of this
  world,
are immersed in this world every day,
ready to hasten to wherever there is a brother or
  sister in need of help,
a tear to be dried, a request for help to be answered.
On this we will be judged.
Amen.

—JOHN PAUL II

FIVE

On Living in the World

At the heart of every culture is its approach to the greatest of all mysteries: the mystery of God.
　　　　　　　　　　　　—JOHN PAUL II

I ask not only on behalf of these, but also on behalf of those who will believe in me through their word, that they may all be one. As you, Father, are in me and I am in you, may they also be in us, so that the world may believe that you have sent me.
　　　　　　　　　　　　—JOHN 17:20–21

e do not live in an irrational or meaningless world. On the contrary, there is a moral logic that is built into human life and that makes dialogue between individuals and people possible. If we want a century of violent coercion to be succeeded by a century of persuasion, we can, and must, find a way to discuss the human future intelligibly. The universal moral law written on the human heart is precisely the kind of "grammar" needed if the world is to engage in this discussion of its future.

However, our world and the events of history cannot be understood in depth without first professing faith in the God who is at work in them. Faith sharpens the inner eye, opening the mind to discover in the flux of events the workings of Providence.

Our modern world, despite its many successes, continues to be marked by contradictions. These include materialism and a growing contempt for human life, which have now assumed disturbing proportions. Many people live their lives with no other allegiance than to the laws of profit, prestige, and power.

But how can we fail to acknowledge with joy the positive aspects of our times? Progress in industry and agriculture has brought a higher standard of living to millions of people and offers great hope for many others. Technology has shrunk distances, while information has become instantaneous and has made possible new advances in human knowledge. Respect for the environment is growing and becoming a way of life. A great army of quiet volunteers, whose generosity often remains hidden, is working tirelessly in every part of the world for the good of humanity, sparing no effort especially in meeting the needs of the poor and the suffering.

However, one of the most disturbing phenomena of the modern world, which can be considered typical of contemporary culture, is drug use and addiction. Drugs are a symptom of a deeper weakness and illness, which especially affects the younger generations who are more exposed to a culture that is poor in genuine values. Drug addiction, with its capacity for damaging a person's willpower, is an obstacle that reveals both the intimate fragility of the human being and our need for help from the world that surrounds us, and—even more radically—from Him who alone can act in the depth of our psyche in times of great difficulty. Relationship with God, lived in an attitude of authentic faith, is an extraordinarily effective support on the journey to recovery from humanly desperate situations.

The near future is also likely to bring new governmental and legal activity regarding humanity's intervention in our personal lives, our bodily nature, and the environment. We are witnessing the birth of biorights and biopolitics. It is all the more important that we are committed to ensuring that this process takes place with respect for humanity's nature, the demands of which are expressed by the natural law.

In the sphere of human rights, it is more appropriate than ever to ask our contemporaries to question themselves on what is mistakenly called "reproductive health." The expression contains a contradiction; actually, it includes the alleged "right to abortion." Thus, it denies the basic right of every human being to life; and in harming one of its members, it injures the whole human race. The roots of the contradiction between the solemn affirmation of human rights and their tragic denial in practice lie in a notion of freedom that exalts the isolated individual in an absolute way, and gives no place to solidarity, openness to others, and service to them.

Recognition of someone as a human being must never be based solely on the awareness or experience we may have of them, but rather on the certitude that they have an infinite value from conception, which comes to them from their relationship with God. Human beings have primacy over the idea others have of them; and their existence is absolute, and not relative.

Science, when separated from the authentic values that define the person, can deteriorate to the level of an experimental exercise to satisfy the law of supply and demand. Instead of responding to our deepest needs, it is limited to producing partial solutions for our immediate requirements. Thus, the intimate connection, which links us with the depths of our being, created in God's image, is cut short. The historical task that unites believers, the men and women of goodwill in scientific research, consists in promoting, beyond all legal convention, that which favors human dignity above all.

The conquest and exploitation of resources has also become predominant and invasive, and today it has even reached the point of threatening the environment's hospitable aspect: the environment as "resource" risks threatening the environment as "home." But technology that pollutes can also cleanse; production that amasses can also distribute justly. The ethic of respect for life and human dignity, for the rights of today's generations and those to come, can prevail.

All of this requires firm points of reference and inspiration, a clear knowledge of creation as a work of God's provident wisdom, and the awareness of human dignity and responsibility in the plan of creation.

This past century has known many martyrs, especially because of Nazism, Communism, and racial or tribal conflicts. People from every sector of society have suffered for their faith, paying with their blood for their fidelity to the Christian message or courageously facing interminable years of imprisonment and privations of every kind because they refused to yield to an ideology that had become a pitiless dictatorial regime.

We need to clarify the essential difference between an unhealthy form of nationalism, which teaches contempt for other nations or cultures, and patriotism, which is a proper love of one's country. True patriotism never seeks to advance the well-being of one's own nation at the expense of others. For in the end, this would harm one's own nation as well: doing wrong damages both aggressor and victim. Nationalism, particularly in its most radical forms, is thus the antithesis of true patriotism; and today we must ensure that extreme nationalism does not continue to give rise to new forms of the aberrations of totalitarianism.

War, even wars that "solve" the problems that cause them, do so only by leaving a wake of victims and destruction, which weighs heavily upon ensuing peace negotiations. Awareness of this should encourage people, nations, and states once and for all to rise above the "culture of war," not only in its most detestable form—namely, the power to wage war used as an instrument of supremacy—but also in the less odious, but no less destructive, form of recourse to arms as an expeditious way to solve a problem. Precisely in a time such as ours, which is familiar with the most sophisticated technologies of destruction, it is urgently necessary to develop a consistent "culture of peace," which will forestall and counter the seemingly inevitable outbreaks of armed violence, including taking steps to stop the growth of the arms industry and of arms trafficking.

Even before this, the sincere desire for peace has to be translated into a firm decision to remove every obstacle to achieving peace. Here, the various religions can make an important contribution, as they have often done in the past, by speaking out against war and bravely facing the consequent risks.

Tolerance is simply not enough, however. Mutual acceptance is not enough. Jesus Christ, He who is and who is to come, expects from us a visible sign of unity, a joint witness.

To believe it is possible to know a universally valid truth is in no way to encourage intolerance. On the contrary, it is the essential condition for sincere and authentic dialogue between people. On this basis alone is it possible to overcome divisions and to journey together toward full truth, walking those paths known only to the Spirit of the Risen Lord.

What kinds of brothers and sisters are we who only tolerate one another? We also need to accept one another. But again, we cannot be content even with mutual acceptance. A great hour is striking. Our reply should be equal to the great moment of this special *kairos* of God.

Solidarity with our brothers and sisters means taking responsibility for those in trouble. For Christians, the migrant or refugee is not merely an individual to be respected in accordance with the norms established by law, but a person whose presence challenges us and whose needs become an obligation for our responsibility. "What have you done for your brother?" The answer should not be limited to what is imposed by law, but should be made in the manner of our compassionate solidarity to one another.

A person—particularly if they are weak, defenseless, driven to the margins of society—is a sacrament of Christ's presence: "I was a stranger and you welcomed me." It is our task not only to present constantly the Lord's teaching of faith and compassion, but also to indicate its appropriate application to the various situations that our changing world continues to create. Today, the illegal migrant and the refugee come before us like that "stranger" in whom Jesus asks to be recognized. To welcome them and to show them solidarity is a duty of hospitality and fidelity to the Christian identity itself.

Our world has yet to learn how to live with diversity. The fact of "difference" and the reality of "the other" can sometimes be felt as a burden, or even as a threat. Amplified by historic grievances and exacerbated by the manipulations of the unscrupulous, the fear of difference can lead to a denial of the very humanity of the other, with the result that people fall into a cycle of violence in which no one is spared, not even the children.

From bitter experience, we know that the fear of difference—especially when it expresses itself in a narrow and exclusive nationalism that denies any rights to the other—can lead to a true nightmare of violence and terror. And yet, if we make the effort to look at matters objectively, we see that there is a fundamental commonality transcending all the differences that distinguish individuals and people. Different cultures are but different ways of facing the question of the meaning of personal existence. And it is precisely here that we find one source of the respect that is due to every culture and every nation. Every culture is an effort to ponder the mystery of the world, and in particular of the human person: it is a way of giving expression to the transcendent dimension of human life. At the heart of every culture is its approach to the greatest of all mysteries: the mystery of God.

To cut oneself off from the reality of "difference" between cultures—or worse, to attempt to stamp out that "difference"—is to cut oneself off from the possibility of sounding the depths of the mystery of human life. The truth about humanity is the unchangeable standard by which all cultures are judged; but every culture has something to teach us about one or another dimension of that complex truth. Thus the "difference" that some find so threatening can, through respectful dialogue, become the source of a deeper understanding of the mystery of human existence.

This life is a talent entrusted to all of us so that we can transform it and increase it, making it a gift to others. No person is an iceberg drifting on the ocean of history. Each one of us belongs to a great family, in which we have our own place and our own role to play. Selfishness can make us deaf and dumb to other people's needs; love opens our eyes and our hearts, enabling us to make the original and irreplaceable contribution that—together with the thousands of deeds of so many of our other brothers and sisters, often distant and unknown—converges to form a mosaic of compassion and charity that can change the tide of history.

The new millennium is posing numerous questions to humanity, but it also offers new and unsuspected opportunities. What will the world of the twenty-first century be like? Shall we be able to make the most of our past experiences and build peaceful coexistence into the heart of each community and among the nations of our world? Will the longing for freedom of so many people of the world be granted? Yes, these problems facing us are immense, but future generations will ask us to account for the way in which we have exercised our responsibilities.

Finally, we can never ignore the transcendent, spiritual dimension of the human experience; can never ignore it without harming the cause of humanity and the cause of human freedom itself. Whatever diminishes humanity—whatever shortens the horizon of humanity's aspiration to goodness—harms the cause of freedom. In order to recover our hope and our trust with the ending of this past century of sorrows, we must regain sight of that transcendent horizon of possibility to which the soul of humanity aspires.

Our visible world is like a road map pointing to heaven, the eternal dwelling of the living God. We must learn to see the Creator by contemplating the beauty of His creation. In this world the goodness, wisdom, and almighty power of God shines forth; and the human intellect can discover the Creator's hand in the wonderful works that He has made. Reason can know God through the book of nature: a personal God who is infinitely good, wise, powerful, and eternal, who transcends our world and, at the same time, is present in the depths of His creatures.

St. Paul writes: "Ever since the creation of the world his eternal power and divine nature, invisible though they are, have been understood and seen through the things he has made." Jesus teaches us to see the Father's hand in the beauty of the lilies of the field, the birds of the air, the starry night, fields ripe for the harvest, the faces of children, and the needs of the poor and humble. If you look at our world with a pure heart, you too will see the face of God because it reveals the mystery of the Creator's provident love.

For God so loved the world that he gave his only Son, so that everyone who believes in him may not perish but may have eternal life.

Indeed, God did not send the Son into the world to condemn the world, but in order that the world might be saved through him.

—JOHN 3:16–17

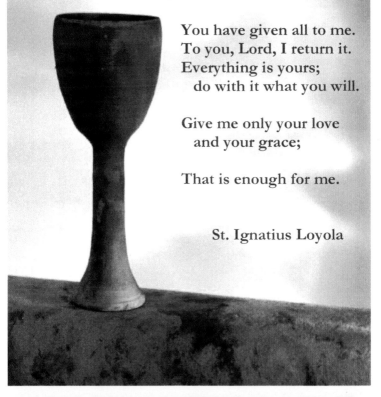

Take, Lord, and receive all my liberty;
My memory, my understanding
And my entire will,
All I have and call my own.

You have given all to me.
To you, Lord, I return it.
Everything is yours;
  do with it what you will.

Give me only your love
  and your grace;

That is enough for me.

St. Ignatius Loyola

LET US ASK THE LORD TO STRENGTHEN
in all Christians faith in Christ, the Savior
of the world.
Listen to us, O Lord.
Let us ask the Lord to sustain and guide
Christians with His gifts along the way to full
unity.
Listen to us, O Lord.
Let us ask the Lord for the gift of unity and
peace for the world.
Listen to us, O Lord.
Let us pray: We ask You, O Lord, for the gifts of
Your Spirit. Enable us to penetrate the depth
of the whole truth, and grant that we may
share with others the goods that You put at our
disposal.
Teach us to overcome divisions. Send us Your
Spirit to lead to full unity Your sons and
daughters in full charity, in obedience to Your
will, through Christ our Lord.
Amen.

—JOHN PAUL II

SIX

On Morality and the Christian Conscience

The examination of conscience is one of the most decisive moments in a person's life. It places each individual before the truth of his or her own life. Thus, we discover the distance that separates our deeds from the ideal that we had set for ourselves.

—JOHN PAUL II

By rejecting conscience, certain persons have suffered shipwreck in the faith.

—1 TIMOTHY 1:19

*M*any of today's problems are the result of a false notion of individual freedom at work in our culture, as if one could be free only when rejecting every objective norm of conduct, refusing to assume responsibility, or even refusing to put curbs on instincts and passions. Instead, true freedom actually implies that we are capable of choosing a good without constraint. This is the truly human way of proceeding in the choices—big and small—that life puts before us.

The fact that we are also able to choose not to act as we see we should is a necessary condition of our moral freedom. But in that case, we must account for the good that we fail to do and for the evil that we commit. Our sense of moral accountability needs to be reawakened if our society is to survive as a civilization built upon justice and solidarity.

Our freedom has been weakened and conditioned in many ways, not least as a consequence of the mysterious and dramatic history of mankind's original rebellion against the Creator's will. But we remain free and responsible beings who have been redeemed by Jesus Christ, and we must educate our freedom to recognize and choose what is right and good, and to reject what does not conform to the original truth concerning our nature and our destiny as God's creatures.

Freedom is not simply the absence of tyranny or oppression. Nor is freedom a license to do whatever we like. Freedom has an inner logic that distinguishes it and ennobles it: freedom is ordered to the truth, and is fulfilled in humanity's quest for truth and in humanity's living the truth.

One of the key problems facing us is the widespread misunderstanding of the role of conscience, whereby individual conscience and experience are exalted above or against Church teaching. The men and women of today's world—who are often victims of educational theories proposing that they "create" their own values and that feeling good about themselves is a primary guiding moral principle—are asking to be led out of this moral confusion.

Those who teach in the name of the Church should fearlessly honor the dignity of the moral conscience as the sanctuary in which the voice of God is heard. But with equal care, they should proclaim, in opposition to all subjectivism, that conscience is not a tribunal that creates the good, but must be formed in the light of universal and objective norms of morality.

Clear teaching on all such matters is liberating because it presents the true meaning of discipleship: Christ calls His followers to friendship with Him. In fact, the personal following of Christ is the essential foundation of Christian morality. The "obedience of faith" is both an intellectual assent to doctrine as well as a life commitment that draws us into ever more-perfect union with

Christ Himself. The Church must always be careful not to reduce "the word of truth" to an abstract code of ethics and morality, or a treatise of rules for good behavior. The preaching of Christian morality must not empty Christ's Cross of its power.

At times in the discussions about new and complex moral problems, it can seem that Christian morality is in itself too demanding, difficult to understand, and almost impossible to practice. This is untrue, since Christian morality consists in the simplicity of its Gospel: that of following Jesus Christ, of abandoning ourselves to Him, and of letting ourselves be transformed by His grace and renewed by His mercy—gifts that come to us in the living communion of His Church.

We must ask ourselves: why do so many acquiesce in attitudes and behaviors that offend human dignity and disfigure the image of God in us? The normal thing would be for conscience to point out the mortal danger to the individual and to humanity contained in the easy acceptance of evil and sin. Is it because conscience itself is losing the ability to distinguish good from evil?

In a technological culture in which people are used to dominating matter—discovering its laws and mechanisms in order to transform it according to their wishes—the danger arises of also wanting to manipulate conscience and its demands. In a culture that holds that no universally valid truths are possible, nothing is absolute. Therefore, in the end—they say—objective goodness and evil no longer really matter. Good comes to mean what is pleasing or useful at a particular moment. Evil means what contradicts our subjective wishes. Each person can build a private system of values.

Conscience is the most secret core and sanctuary of a person, where we are alone with God. In the depths of our conscience, we detect the moral law, which does not impose itself upon us, but which holds us to a higher obedience. This law is not an external human law, but the voice of God, calling us to free ourselves from the grip of evil desires and sin, and stimulating us to seek what is good and true in life.

Moral truth is objective, and a properly formed conscience can perceive it. But if conscience itself has been corrupted, how can it be restored? If conscience—which is light—no longer enlightens, how can we overcome the moral darkness?

The examination of conscience is one of the most decisive moments in a person's life. It places each individual before the truth of his or her own life. Thus, we discover the distance that separates our deeds from the ideal that we had set for ourselves.

Jesus says: "The eye is the lamp of the body. So, if your eye is healthy, your whole body will be full of light; but if your eye is unhealthy, your whole body will be full of darkness. If then the light in you is darkness, how great is the darkness!" But Jesus also says: "I am the light of the world. Whoever follows me will never walk in darkness but will have the light of life."

If you follow Christ, you will restore your conscience to its rightful place and proper role, and you will be the light of the world, the salt of the earth. A rebirth of conscience must come from two sources: first, the effort to know objective truth with certainty, including the truth about God; and second, the light of faith in Jesus Christ, who alone has the words of life.

The guarantee that objective truth exists is found
in God, who is absolute Truth. Objectively speaking, the search for truth and the search for God
are one and the same. Every individual has the
grave duty to form his own conscience in the
light of that objective truth which everyone
can come to know, and which no one may be
prevented from knowing. To claim that one has
a right to act according to conscience—but without at the same time acknowledging the duty
to conform one's conscience to the truth and
to the law, which God Himself has written on
our hearts—in the end means nothing more
than imposing one's limited personal opinion
on others.

On the contrary, the truth must be passionately pursued and lived to the best of one's ability.
Freedom of conscience, rightly understood, is by its
very nature always ordered to the truth.

Faced with the obligation of following their
own consciences in the search for the truth, the
disciples of Jesus Christ know that they must not
trust only in their personal capacity for moral discernment. Revelation enlightens their consciences
and enables them to know the freedom that is

God's great gift to mankind. Not only has He inscribed the natural law within the heart of each of us, in "man's most secret core and his sanctuary [w]here he is alone with God," but He has also revealed His own law in the Scriptures. Here we find the call, or rather the command, to love God and to observe His law.

The Church's teaching, and particularly her firmness in defending the universal and permanent validity of precepts prohibiting intrinsically evil acts, is sometimes seen as the sign of an intolerable intransigence, particularly with regard to the enormously complex and conflict-filled situations present in the moral life of individuals and of society and our world today. The Church, we hear, is lacking in understanding and compassion.

But the Church can never, in fact, be separated from her teaching mission. As teacher, the Church never tires of proclaiming the moral norm. The Church is in no way the author or the arbiter of this norm. In obedience to the truth that is Christ, whose image is reflected in the nature and dignity of the human person, the Church interprets the moral norm and proposes it to all people of goodwill, without concealing its demands of radicalness and perfection.

In fact, genuine understanding and compassion must mean love for the person, for her true good, for our authentic freedom. And this does not result, certainly, from concealing or weakening moral truth, but rather from proposing it in its most profound meaning as an outpouring of God's eternal wisdom, which we have received in Christ, and as a service to humanity, to the growth of our freedom, and to the attainment of our happiness. Still, a clear and forceful presentation of moral truth can never be separated from a profound and heartfelt respect, born of that patient and trusting love that humanity always needs along our moral journey, a journey frequently wearisome on account of difficulties, weakness, and painful situations.

It is appropriate that, as the third millennium of Christianity dawns, the Church should also become more fully conscious of the sinfulness of her own children, recalling all those times in history when they departed from the spirit of Christ and His Gospel and, instead of offering to the world the witness of a life inspired by the values of faith, indulged in ways of thinking and acting that were truly forms of counterwitness and scandal.

Although she is holy because of her incorporation into Christ, the Church does not tire of doing penance before God and man; and she acknowledges her own sinful sons and daughters.

It is also fitting that the Church should make its next millennial passage with a clear awareness of what has happened to her during the last ten centuries. She cannot cross the threshold of this new millennium without encouraging her children to purify themselves, through repentance, of past errors and instances of infidelity, inconsistency, and slowness to act. Acknowledging the weaknesses of the past is an act of honesty and courage that helps us to strengthen our faith, which alerts us to face today's temptations and challenges, and prepares us to meet them.

With the start of this new millennium, Christians need to place themselves humbly before the Lord and examine themselves for the responsibility that they, too, have for the evils of our day.

How can we remain silent, for example, about the religious indifference that causes many people today to live as if God did not exist, or to be content with a vague religiosity, incapable of coming

to grips with the question of truth and the requirement of consistency? To this must be added the
widespread loss of the transcendent sense of human
life and confusion in the moral and ethical sphere,
even about the most fundamental values of respect
for life and the family.

The sons and daughters of the Church need to
examine themselves in this regard. To what extent
have we been shaped by the climate of secularism
and ethical relativism? And what responsibility do
we bear, in view of the increasing lack of religion,
for not having shown the true face of God in our
religious, moral, or social lives? For many of us, the
spiritual life is passing through a time of uncer-
tainty that affects not only our moral lives but also
our lives of prayer and the theological correctness
of our faith.

We should all take to heart the message of the
Gospel parable of the Pharisee and the tax collector. The tax collector might possibly have had some
justification for the sins he committed, such as to
diminish his responsibility. Yet, his prayer does not
dwell on such justifications, but rather on his own
unworthiness before God's infinite holiness: "God,
be merciful to me, a sinner!" The Pharisee, on the

other hand, is self-justified, finding some excuse for each of his failings.

Here we encounter two different attitudes of the moral conscience of humanity in every age. The tax collector represents a repentant conscience, fully aware of the frailty of its own nature, and seeing in its own failings, whatever their subjective justifications, a confirmation of its need for redemption. The Pharisee represents a self-satisfied conscience, under the illusion that it is able to observe the law without the help of grace and convinced that it does not need mercy.

All of us must take great care not to allow ourselves to be tainted by the attitude of the Pharisee, which would seek to eliminate awareness of our limits and our sin. In our day, this attitude is expressed particularly in the attempt to adapt the moral norm to one's own capacities and personal interests, and even in the rejection of the very idea of a norm.

So let us remember: it is only by listening to the voice of God in our most intimate being, and by acting in accordance with its directions, that we will reach the freedom we yearn for. As Jesus said, only the truth can make us free. And the truth is not the fruit of each individual's imagination. God gave us intelligence to know the truth and the will to achieve what is morally good. He has given us the light of conscience to guide our moral decisions—and, above all, to love good and avoid evil.

Pray for us; we are sure that we have a clear conscience, desiring to act honorably in all things.

—HEBREWS 13:18

HOLY SPIRIT AND SEAT OF WISDOM,
help us in the great endeavor that we are
    carrying out
to meet on a more and more mature way
our brothers and sisters in the faith.
Through all the means of knowledge, of mutual
    respect, of love,
may we be able to rediscover gradually the
    divine plan.
Teach us constantly the ways that lead
    to unity.
Help us all to proclaim Christ and reveal the
    power of God
and the wisdom of God hidden in His Cross.
How greatly I desire to entrust to You
all the difficult problems of the societies,
    systems, and states—
problems that cannot be solved with hatred, war,
    and self-destruction,
but only by peace, justice, and respect for the
    rights of people and nations.
Amen.

—JOHN PAUL II

SEVEN

On the Church

The Church was born on the day of Pentecost, when the Spirit came upon Christ's followers; the Spirit is the One who empowers the Church to be a sacrament of Christ's life in the world.
—JOHN PAUL II

꘎

And I tell you, you are Peter, and on this rock I will build my church, and the gates of Hades will not prevail against it. I will give you the keys of the kingdom of heaven, and whatever you bind on earth will be bound in heaven, and whatever you loose on earth will be loosed in heaven.
—MATTHEW 16:18–19

s we look at today's world, we are struck by many negative factors that can lead to pessimism. But this feeling is unjustified, if we have faith in God our Father and Lord, and in His goodness and mercy. As we enter the third millennium of the Redemption, God is preparing a great springtime for Christianity, and we can already see its first signs. In fact, both in the non-Christian world and in the traditionally Christian world, people are gradually drawing closer to

Gospel ideals and values, a development that the Church seeks to encourage. Today there is a new consensus among people about these values: the rejection of violence and war; respect for the human person and for human rights; the desire for freedom, justice, and brotherhood; the surmounting of different forms of racism and nationalism; and the affirmation of the dignity and role of women.

Now at the dawning of the third millennium, the Church once more intends to ponder the very essence of her divine-human constitution and of that mission which enables her to share in the messianic mission of Christ. Following this line, we can go back to the Upper Room, where Jesus Christ reveals the Holy Spirit as the Paraclete, the Spirit of truth, and where He speaks of His own departure through the Cross as the necessary condition for the Spirit's coming: "It is to your advantage that I go away, for if I do not go away, the Advocate will not come to you; but if I go, I will send him to you." This prediction first came true the evening of Easter day, and then during the celebration of Pentecost in Jerusalem, and ever since then it is being fulfilled in human history through the Church.

In the light of that prediction, we also grasp the full meaning of what Jesus says at the Last Supper about His new coming. For it is significant that in the same farewell discourse Jesus foretells not only His departure, but His new coming as well. His exact words are: "I will not leave you orphaned; I am coming to you." And at the moment of His final farewell before He ascends into heaven, He repeats even more explicitly: "And remember, I am with you always, to the end of the age."

This new coming of Christ occurs by the power of the Holy Spirit, who makes it possible for Christ, who has gone away, to come now and forever in a new way. This new coming of Christ through the power of the Holy Spirit and His constant presence and action in the spiritual life are accomplished in the sacramental reality. In this reality, Christ, who has gone away in His visible humanity, comes, is present, and acts in the Church in such an intimate way as to make it His own Body. As such, the Church lives, works, and grows "to the end of the age." And all of this happens through the power of the Holy Spirit.

According to our faith, the Word of God became flesh and came to dwell in the world. By conquering evil and the power of sin through His death on the Cross, and by His loving obedience, He brought salvation to all, and became reconciliation for all. In Him, God reconciled man to Himself.

The Church has the mission of proclaiming this reconciliation and of being its sacrament in the world. The Church *is* the sacrament—the sign and means of reconciliation. The Church is a sacrament by her very existence as a reconciled community that witnesses to and represents the work of Christ in the world.

She is also a sacrament through her service as the custodian and interpreter of sacred Scripture, which is the Good News of reconciliation, and tells each succeeding generation about God's loving plan and shows to each generation the paths to universal reconciliation in Christ.

Finally, she is a sacrament by reason of the seven sacraments. For since they commemorate and renew Christ's Paschal Mystery, all the sacraments are a source of life for the Church, and in the Church's hands they are a means of conversion to God and of reconciliation among people.

The mission of reconciliation is proper to the whole Church, and especially to that Church which has already been admitted to the full sharing in divine glory with the Virgin Mary—the angels and the saints, who contemplate and adore the thrice-holy God. The Church in heaven, the Church on earth, and the Church in purgatory are mysteriously united in this cooperation with Christ in reconciling the world to God.

The first means of this saving action is that of prayer. The Blessed Virgin and the saints—who have now reached the end of their earthly journey and possess God's glory—sustain by their intercession their brethren, who are on pilgrimage through the world, in the commitment to conversion, to faith, to getting up again after every fall, to acting in order to help the growth of communion and peace in the Church and in the world. In the mystery of the communion of saints, universal reconciliation is accomplished in its most profound form, which is also the most fruitful for the salvation of all.

There is yet another means: that of preaching. The Church, as mother and teacher, untiringly exhorts people to reconciliation. And she does not hesitate to condemn the evil of sin, to proclaim the need for conversion, to invite and ask people to be reconciled. In fact, this is her prophetic mission in today's world, just as it was in the world of yesterday. It is the same mission as that of her teacher and head, Jesus. Like Him, the Church will always carry out this mission with sentiments of merciful love and will bring to all people those words of forgiveness and that invitation to hope which come from the Cross.

There is also the often difficult and demanding means of pastoral action aimed at bringing back every individual—whoever and wherever that person may be—to the path, at times a long one, leading back to the Father in the communion of all the brethren.

Also, there is the means of witness, which is almost always silent. This witness cannot fail to assume two fundamental aspects. This first aspect is that of being the sign of that universal charity which Jesus Christ left as an inheritance to His followers, as a proof of belonging to His Kingdom. The second aspect is the translation into ever-new manifestations of conversion and reconciliation, both within the Church and outside it, by the overcoming of tensions, by mutual forgiveness, by growth in the spirit of brotherhood and peace that is to be spread throughout the world. By this means, the Church will effectively be able to work for the creation of what Paul VI called the "civilization of love."

The ecclesial community, while always having a universal dimension, finds its most immediate and visible expression in the parish. It is there that the Church is seen locally. In a certain sense, it is the Church living in the midst of the homes of her sons and daughters.

It is necessary that, in light of the faith, all rediscover the true meaning of the parish; that is, the place where the very mystery of the Church is present and at work, even if at times it might be scattered over vast territories or almost not to be found in crowded and chaotic modern sections of cities. The parish is not principally a structure, a territory, or a building, but rather "the family of God, a fellowship afire with a unifying spirit."

Plainly and simply, the parish is founded on a theological reality because it is a Eucharistic community. This means that the parish is a community properly suited for celebrating the Eucharist, the living source for its building up and the sacramental bond of its being in full communion with the whole Church. Such suitableness is rooted in the fact that the parish is a community of faith, an organic community, that is constituted by the ordained ministers and other Christians, in which the pastor—who represents the diocesan bishop—is the hierarchical bond with the entire particular Church.

In our present circumstances, the lay faithful have the ability to do much in their parishes in order to reawaken missionary zeal toward nonbelievers and believers themselves who have abandoned the faith or grown lax in the Christian life.

If indeed the parish is the Church placed in the neighborhoods of humanity, it lives and is at work through being deeply inserted in human society and intimately bound up with its aspirations and its dramatic events. Oftentimes, the social context, especially in certain countries and environments, is violently shaken by elements of disintegration and dehumanization. The individual is lost and disoriented, but there always remains in the human heart the desire to experience and cultivate caring and personal relationships.

The response to such a desire can come from the parish, when, with the lay faithful's participation, it adheres to its fundamental vocation and mission, that is, to be a place in the world for the community of believers to gather together as a sign and instrument of the vocation of all to communion: in a word, to be a house of welcome to all and a place of service to all, or, as Pope John XXIII was fond of saying, to be the "village fountain" to which all would have recourse in their thirst.

In order to overcome conflicts and to ensure that normal tensions do not prove harmful to the unity of the Church, we must all apply ourselves to the Word of God. We must relinquish our own subjective views and seek the truth where it is to be found, namely in the Divine Word itself and in the authentic interpretation of that Word provided by the Church. In this light, listening to one another with respect; refraining from hasty judgments; being patient; the ability to avoid subordinating the faith that unites to the opinions, fashions, and ideological choices that divide: these are all qualities of a dialogue within the Church that must be persevering, open, and sincere.

The Church asks us to go, in the power of the Holy Spirit, to those who are near and those who

are far away. Share with them the freedom we have
found in Christ. People thirst for genuine inner
freedom. They yearn for the life that Christ came
to give in abundance. The world of the new millennium is like a field ready for the harvest. Christ
needs laborers ready to work in His vineyard. May
we not fail Him. In our hands, let us carry the
Cross of Christ. On our lips, let us speak the words
of life. And in our hearts, let us share the saving
grace of the Lord.

There is no authentic Christianity if there is
no mission activity; Jesus is a gift from God that
must be brought to everyone. Certainly, not everyone is called to set out on mission; and it is not as
important where, but how. We can be authentic
apostles, in a most fruitful way, at home, at work,
in a hospital, in a convent cloister. What counts is
that the heart burns with that divine charity which
alone is able to transform into light, fire, and new
life not only physical and moral sufferings, but
also our daily fatigue.

    Seeing the many people who have not yet been
reached by the Good News of salvation, Christians
cannot fail to note in their hearts the urgency that
shook the apostle Paul, causing him to cry out,

"Woe to me if I do not proclaim the gospel!" To a certain degree, in fact, each of us is personally responsible, before God, for those millions of people who are without faith.

The size of the task and the recognition of the inadequacy of one's own energies may at times lead to discouragement, but we need not fear: we are not alone. The Lord Himself reassures us: "I am with you always."

Humanity's future depends on persons who rely on the truth and whose lives are enlightened by moral principles that enable their hearts to love to the point of sacrifice. The model of such a loving servant is Jesus Christ. This is the Church's constant proclamation to the world: Jesus Christ, the same yesterday, today, and forever.

Do not cease to proclaim that Jesus Christ is the only Savior, that His gospel can transform minds and hearts, bring about the desired reconciliation, and call all the earth's people to true brotherhood devoid of hatred or distrust. We must be Christians who are familiar with the revealed Word, with the Church's social and moral teaching, as well as with the demands of justice and peace; committed to the service of charity; diligent in bringing together all of our brothers and sisters, with respect for their different ways of thinking.

Through His sacrifice, Jesus desired that down through the centuries, we all should hear His voice of truth. This is why He entrusted to the Eleven, with Peter as head, and to their successors the mission to watch like sentries so that the *una, sancta, catholica, et apostolica Ecclesia* [the one, holy, Catholic, and apostolic Church] might be realized in each of the particular Churches entrusted to them. Thus in the communion of pastors with the bishop of Rome, there is achieved the witness to truth that is also a service to unity, in which the role of the successor of Peter has a very special place.

At the dawning of this third millennium, how can we not invoke for all Christians the grace of that unity merited for them by the Lord Jesus at so high a price? The unity of faith, in adherence to revealed Truth; the unity of hope, in the journey toward the fulfillment of God's Kingdom; the unity of charity, with its multiple forms and applications in all areas of human life: in this unity all conflicts can be resolved, and all separated Christians can find reconciliation in order to reach the goal of full and visible communion.

And should we ask if all this is possible, the answer will always be "yes." It is the same answer that Mary of Nazareth heard: "For nothing will be impossible with God."

Only in Christ can men and women find answers to the ultimate questions that trouble them. Only in Christ can they fully understand their dignity as persons created and loved by God. Jesus Christ is the "father's only son, full of grace and truth."

By keeping the Incarnation of the eternal Word before her eyes, the Church understands more fully her twofold nature—human and divine. She is the mystical Body of the Word made flesh. As such, she is inseparably united with her Lord and is holy in a way that can never fail.

The Church is also the visible means that God uses to reconcile sinful humanity to Himself. She is the people of God making its pilgrim way to the Father's house. In this sense, she is constantly in need of conversion and renewal, and her members must ever be challenged "to purify and renew themselves so that the sign of Christ can shine more brightly on her face." Only when the Church generates works of genuine holiness and humble service, do the words of Isaiah come true: "all the nations shall stream to it."

The Church needs us to enlighten the world and to show it the path to life. The challenge is to make the Church's "yes" to life concrete and effective. The struggle will be long, and it needs each one of us. Place your intelligence, your talents, your enthusiasm, your compassion, and your fortitude in the service of life.

Have no fear. The outcome of the battle for life is already decided, even though the struggle goes on against great odds and with much suffering. The paradox of the Christian message is this: Christ—the Head—has already conquered sin and death. Christ in his Body—the pilgrim People of God—continually suffers the onslaught of the evil one and all the evil of which sinful humanity is capable.

At this stage of history, the liberating message of the Gospel of Life has been put into our hands. And the mission of proclaiming it to the ends of the earth is now passing to the next generation. Like the great apostle Paul, we too must feel the full urgency of the task. The Church needs our energies, our enthusiasm, our ideals, in order to make the Gospel of Life penetrate the fabric of society, transforming people's hearts and the structures of society in order to create a civilization of true justice and love.

I therefore, the prisoner in the Lord, beg you to lead a life worthy of the calling to which you have been called, with all humility and gentleness, with patience, bearing with one another in love, making every effort to maintain the unity of the Spirit in the bond of peace. There is one body and one Spirit, just as you were called to the one hope of your calling, one Lord, one faith, one baptism, one God and Father of all, who is above all and through all and in all.

—EPHESIANS 4:1–6

A PARISH PRAYER

May spouses pray for the grace of perseverance in
conjugal faithfulness.
May parents pray to obtain the love necessary to
carry out their vocation
as received from God.
May children find in their parish a vaster
family home.
May the young seek in their parish support for
their ideals
and commit themselves with readiness to serve
God and man.
May the sick and the suffering find consolation
and relief.
May all in the parish become aware of being
members of the Body of Christ
and realize that the kingdom of God is
approaching—
that, in fact, it is already present.
We pray for all this, trusting above all in the
intercession of Mary,
who is Mother of the Church and the cause of
our joy.
Amen.

—JOHN PAUL II

EIGHT

On the Eucharist and the Mass

Indeed, the Eucharist is the ineffable sacrament—the essential commitment and, above all, the visible grace and source of supernatural strength for the Church.

—John Paul II

༺ꗊ༻

For I received from the Lord what I also handed on to you, that the Lord Jesus on the night when he was betrayed took a loaf of bread, and when he had given thanks, he broke it, and said, "This is my body that is for you. Do this in remembrance of me." In the same way he took the cup also, after supper, saying, "This cup is the new covenant in my blood. Do this, as often as you drink it, in remembrance of me." For as often as you eat this bread and drink the cup, you proclaim the Lord's death until he comes.

—1 Corinthians 11:23–26

$\mathcal{I}$n the mystery of the Redemption, the Church not only shares in the Gospel of her Master through fidelity to the word and service of truth, but she also shares in the power of His redeeming action expressed and enshrined by Him in a sacramental form, especially in the Eucharist. The Eucharist is the center and summit of the whole of sacramental life, through which each Christian receives the saving power of the Redemption, beginning with the mystery of Baptism, in which we are buried into the death of Christ in order to become sharers in His Resurrection.

In the light of this, we see more clearly the reason why the entire sacramental life of the Church and of each Christian reaches its summit and fullness in the Eucharist. There is in this sacrament a continual renewing of the mystery of the sacrifice of Himself that He offered to the Father on the altar of the Cross. This is a sacrifice that the Father accepted, giving, in return for this total self-giving by His Son, His own paternal gift and the granting of new immortal life in the Resurrection. This new life, which involves the bodily glorification of the crucified Christ, became an effective sign of the gift granted to humanity, the gift that is the Holy Spirit, through whom the divine life that the Father has in Himself and gives to His Son is communicated to all men and women who are united with Christ.

The Eucharist is the source of the Christian life because whoever shares in it receives the motivation and strength to live as a true Christian. Christ's sacrifice on the Cross imparts to the believer the dynamism of His generous love; the Eucharistic banquet nourishes the faithful with the Body and Blood of the divine Lamb sacrificed for them, and it gives them the strength to follow in His footsteps.

The Eucharist is the summit of the whole Christian life because the faithful bring to it all their prayers and good works, their joys and sufferings. Our modest offerings are then united to the perfect sacrifice of Christ, and are thus completely sanctified and lifted up to God in an act of perfect worship that brings the faithful into the divine intimacy.

The Mass truly makes present the sacrifice of the Cross. Under the species of bread and wine, upon which has been invoked the outpouring of the Spirit who works with absolutely unique power in the words of consecration, Christ offers Himself again to the Father in the same act of sacrifice by which He offered Himself on the Cross.

The Eucharist is not only a particularly intense expression of the reality of the Church's life, but also, in a sense, is its fountainhead. The Eucharist feeds and forms the Church: "Because there is one bread, we who are many are one body, for we all partake of the one bread." Because of this vital link with the sacrament of the Body and Blood of the Lord, the mystery of the Church is savored, proclaimed, and lived supremely in the Eucharist.

At Sunday Mass, Christians relive with particular intensity the experience of the apostles on the evening of Easter when the Risen Lord appeared to them as they were gathered together. In a sense, the People of God of all times were present in that small nucleus of disciples, the first fruits of the Church. Through their testimony, every generation of believers hears the greeting of Christ, rich with the messianic gift of peace, won by His Blood and offered with His Spirit: "Peace be with you."

Sunday is our weekly Easter, recalling and making present the day upon which Christ rose from the dead. It is also the day that reveals the meaning of time. It has nothing in common with the cosmic cycles according to which natural religion and human culture tend to impose a structure on time, succumbing perhaps to the myth of eternal return. The Christian Sunday is wholly other. Springing from the Resurrection, it cuts through human time—the months, the years, the centuries—like a directional arrow that points them towards their target: Christ's Second Coming. Sunday foreshadows the last day, the day of the Parousia, which in a way is already anticipated by Christ's glory in the event of the Resurrection.

In fact, everything that will happen until the end of the world will be no more than an extension and unfolding of what happened on the day when the battered body of the crucified Lord was raised by the power of the Spirit and became in turn the wellspring of the Spirit for all humanity. Christians know that there is no need to wait for another time of salvation, since, however long the world may last, they are already living in the last times.

In celebrating the Eucharist, the community opens itself to communion with the universal Church, imploring the Father to "remember the Church throughout the world" and make her grow in the unity of all the faithful with the pope and with the pastors of the particular Churches, until love is brought to perfection.

For the faithful who have understood the meaning of what they have done, the Eucharistic celebration does not stop at the church door. Like the first witnesses of the Resurrection, Christians who gather each Sunday to experience and proclaim the presence of the Risen Lord are called to evangelize and bear witness in their daily lives. Once the assembly disperses, Christ's disciples return to their everyday surroundings with the commitment to make their whole life a gift, a spiritual sacrifice pleasing to God.

A parish's vocation can be defined only according to the Church's sacramental structure. It is here that Christ's presence in the Paschal Mystery is visibly signified. At Mass, the offerings of all converge: of happiness and suffering, of apostolic efforts and fraternal services of all kinds. The Lord associates the sacrifices of His brothers and sisters with His own sacrifice. He gathers us in His Holy Spirit, He strengthens our faith and our charity, He listens to our petitions to the Father to extend reconciliation, salvation, and peace to the whole world, and He unites us with the saints of every age as we wait for full communion in His Kingdom.

The Lord's Day—as Sunday was called from apostolic times—has always been accorded special attention in the history of the Church because of its close connection with the very core of the Christian mystery. In fact, in the weekly reckoning of time, Sunday recalls the day of Christ's resurrection. It is Easter, which returns week by week, celebrating Christ's victory over sin and death, the fulfillment in Him of the first creation, and the dawn of "a new creation." In commemorating the day of Christ's resurrection, not just once a year, but every Sunday, the Church seeks to indicate to every generation the true fulcrum of history, to which the mystery of the world's origin and its final destiny leads.

Why not make the Lord's Day a more intense time of sharing, encouraging all the inventiveness of which Christian charity is capable? Inviting to a meal people who are alone, visiting the sick, providing food for needy families, spending a few hours in voluntary work and acts of solidarity: these would certainly be ways of bringing into people's lives the love of Christ received at the Eucharistic table.

"I am with you always, to the end of the age." This promise of Christ never ceases to resound in the Church as the fertile secret of her life and the wellspring of her hope. As the day of Resurrection, Sunday is not only the remembrance of a past event: it is a celebration of the living presence of the Risen Lord in the midst of His own people.

For this presence to be properly proclaimed and lived, it is not enough that the disciples of Christ pray individually and commemorate the death and resurrection of Christ inwardly, in the secrecy of their hearts. Those who have received the grace of Baptism are not saved as individuals alone, but as members of the Mystical Body, having become part of the People of God. It is important, therefore, that they come together to express fully the very identity of the Church, the *Ecclesia*, the assembly

called together by the Risen Lord who offered His
life to reunite "the dispersed children of God."

The Church lives by the Eucharist, by the fullness of this sacrament, the stupendous content and
meaning of which have often been expressed in the
Church from the most distant times down to our
own days. And though this teaching is sustained by
the acuteness of theologians, by men and women of
deep faith and prayer, and by ascetics and mystics—
in complete fidelity to the Eucharistic mystery—it
remains incapable of grasping and translating into
words what the Eucharist is in all its fullness, what
is expressed by it and what is actuated by it.

Indeed, the Eucharist is the ineffable sacrament—
the essential commitment and, above all, the visible
grace and source of supernatural strength for the
Church. With all the greater reason, then, it is not
permissible for us, in thought, life, or action, to take
away from this truly most holy sacrament its full
magnitude and its essential meaning. It is at one and
the same time a Sacrifice-sacrament, a Communion-
sacrament, and a Presence-sacrament. And although
it is true that the Eucharist always was and must
continue to be the most profound revelation of
the human brotherhood of Christ's disciples and

confessors, it cannot be treated merely as an occasion for manifesting this brotherhood. When celebrating the sacrament of the Body and Blood of the Lord, the full magnitude of the divine mystery must be respected—as must the full meaning of this sacramental sign in which Christ is really present and is received, the soul is filled with grace, and the pledge of future glory is given.

The Kingdom of God becomes present in the celebration of the sacrament of the Eucharist, which is the Lord's Sacrifice. In this celebration, the fruits of the earth and the work of human hands—the bread and wine—are transformed mysteriously, but really and substantially, through the power of the Holy Spirit and the words of the minister, into the Body and Blood of the Lord Jesus Christ, the Son of God and Son of Mary, through whom the Kingdom of the Father has been made present in our midst.

The goods of this world and the work of our hands—the bread and wine—serve for the coming of the definitive Kingdom, since the Lord, through His Spirit, takes them up into Himself in order to offer Himself to the Father and to offer us with Himself in the renewal of His one Sacrifice, which anticipates God's Kingdom and proclaims its final coming.

Thus the Lord unites us with Himself through the Eucharist—Sacrament and Sacrifice—and He unites us with Himself and with one another by a bond stronger than any natural union. Thus united, He sends us into the whole world to bear witness, through faith and works, to God's love, preparing the coming of His Kingdom and anticipating it, though in the obscurity of the present time.

Eucharistic worship constitutes the soul of all Christian life. In fact, Christian life is expressed in the fulfilling of the greatest commandment, that is to say, in the love of God and neighbor, and this love finds its source in the Blessed Sacrament, which is commonly called the sacrament of love.

The Eucharist signifies this charity, and therefore recalls it, makes it present, and, at the same time, brings it about. Every time that we consciously share in it, there opens in our souls a real dimension of that unfathomable love that includes everything that God has done and continues to do for us human beings; as Christ says: "My Father is still working, and I also am working."

Together with this unfathomable and free gift, which is charity revealed in its fullest degree in the saving sacrifice of the Son of God—the sacrifice of which the Eucharist is the indelible sign—there also springs up within us a lively response of love. We not only know love; we ourselves begin to love. We enter upon the path of love, and along this path make progress.

Thanks to the Eucharist, the love that springs up within us becomes deeper and grows stronger. Eucharistic worship is therefore precisely the expression of that love which is the authentic and deepest characteristic of the Christian vocation. This worship springs from the love and serves the love to which we are all called in Jesus Christ.

A living fruit of this worship is the perfecting of the image of God that we bear within us, an image that corresponds to the one that Christ has revealed in us. As we thus become adorers of the Father "in spirit and truth"—who then mature to an ever-fuller union with Christ—we are ever more united to Him, ever more in harmony with Him.

The authentic sense of the Eucharist becomes the school of active love for our neighbor. We know that this is the true and full order of love that the Lord has taught us: "By this everyone will know that you are my disciples, if you have love for one another." The Eucharist educates us to this love in a deeper way: it shows us, in fact, what value each person, our brother or sister, has in God's eyes, if Christ offers Himself equally to each one, under the species of bread and wine. If our Eucharistic worship is authentic, it must make us grow in awareness of the dignity of each person. The awareness of that dignity becomes the deepest motive of our relationship with our neighbor.

We must also become particularly sensitive to all human suffering and misery, to all injustice and wrong, and seek the way to redress them effectively. Let us learn to discover with respect the truth about the inner self that becomes the dwelling place of God in the Eucharist. Christ comes into the hearts of our brothers and sisters and visits their consciences.

How the image of each and every one changes when we become aware of this reality. This sense of the Eucharistic mystery leads us to a love for our neighbor, to a love for every human being.

Our community has the duty to make the Eucharist the place where fraternity becomes practical solidarity, where the last are the first in the minds and attentions of the brethren, where Christ Himself—through the generous gifts from the rich to the very poor—may somehow prolong in time the miracle of the multiplication of the loaves.

The Eucharist is the full realization of the worship that humanity owes to God, and it cannot be compared to any other religious experience. The Risen Lord calls the faithful together to give them the light of His Word and the nourishment of His Body as the perennial sacramental wellspring of redemption. The grace flowing from this wellspring renews humanity, life, and history.

The Lord is the strength of his people;
   he is the saving refuge of his anointed.
O save your people, and bless your heritage;
   be their shepherd, and carry them forever.

—PSALM 28:8–9

LET US PRAY FOR OUR SPIRITUAL FAMILIES
Let us pray particularly for those who in a
   special way
expect our prayers and are in need of them.
May our fidelity to prayer ensure that Christ will
   become ever more the life of our souls.
O great Sacrament of Faith, O holy Redeemer of
   the World.
Lord Jesus Christ, how grateful we are to You
for having brought us into communion with You,
for having made us one community around You,
for allowing us to celebrate Your sacrifice and
   sacred mysteries
in every place: at the altar, in the confessional,
   the pulpit, the sickroom,
the prisons, the classroom, the lecture hall, the
   offices where we work.
All praise to the Most Holy Eucharist!
Amen.

—JOHN PAUL II

NINE

On the Family

If we are to bring healing to a world so deeply loved by the Father, we cannot neglect to care for the family, the foundation of society.

—John Paul II

✦

*Unless the Lord builds the house,
those who build it labor in vain.*

—Psalm 127:1

*T*hroughout the world, the family is being shaken to its roots. The consequences for individuals and society in personal and collective instability and unhappiness are incalculable. Yet, it is heartening to know that in the face of this extraordinary challenge many Christians are committing themselves to the defense and support of family life.

So often, the pressures of modern living separate husbands and wives from one another, threatening their lifelong interdependence in love and fidelity. Can we also not be concerned about the impact of cultural pressures upon relations between the generations, upon parental authority and the transmission of sacred values? Our Christian conscience should be deeply concerned about the way in which sins against love and against life are often presented as examples of "progress" and emancipation. Most often, they are simply the age-old forms of selfishness dressed up in a new language and presented in a new cultural framework.

The gospel of the Kingdom of God is open to every aspect of earthly progress that helps people to discover and enter the space of divine life, the space of eternal salvation. This is the work of the Church; this is the work that the Holy Spirit will accomplish through all of us, if only we will heed the truth He reveals and be confirmed in His goodness.

In practical terms, there can be no life worthy of the human person without a culture—and a legal system—that honors and defends marriage and the family. The well-being of individuals and communities depends on the healthy state of the family.

Society must strongly reaffirm the right of the child to grow up in a family where, as far as possible, both parents are present. Fathers of families must accept their full share of responsibility for the lives and upbringing of their children. Both parents must spend time with their children and be personally interested in their moral and religious education. Children need not only material support from their parents, but more importantly a secure, affectionate, and morally correct family environment.

In my visits to the Church in every part of the world, I have been deeply moved by the almost universal conditions of difficulty in which young people grow up and live. Too many sufferings are visited upon them by natural calamities, famines, epidemics; by economic and political crises; by the atrocities of wars. And where material conditions are at least adequate, other obstacles arise, not the least of which is the breakdown of family values and stability. In developed countries, a serious moral crisis is already affecting the lives of many young people, leaving them adrift, often without hope, and conditioned to look only for instant gratification.

Yet everywhere there are young men and women deeply concerned about the world around them, ready to give the best of themselves in service to others and particularly sensitive to life's transcendent meaning. But how do we help them? Only by instilling a high moral vision can a society ensure that its young people are given the possibility to mature as free and intelligent human beings, endowed with a robust sense of responsibility for the common good, capable of working with others to create a community and a nation with a strong moral fiber.

Children very soon learn about life. They watch and imitate the behavior of adults. They rapidly learn love and respect for others, but they also quickly absorb the poison of violence and hatred. Family experiences strongly condition the attitudes that children will assume as adults. Consequently, if the family is the place where children first encounter the world, the family must be for children the first school of peace.

How important are children in the eyes of Jesus? We could say that the gospel is full of truth about children. The whole of the gospel could actually be read as the "Gospel of children." We read in the Scripture: "Unless you change and become like children, you will never enter the kingdom of heaven." Is not Jesus pointing to children as models even for grown-ups? In children, there is something that must never be missing in people who want to enter the kingdom of heaven. People who are destined to go to heaven are simple like children, and—like children—are full of trust, rich in goodness, and pure. Only people of this sort can find in God a Father and, thanks to Jesus, can become in their own turn children of God.

Jesus and Mary often choose children to do important tasks for the life of the Church and of humanity. Jesus seems to share with them His concern for others: for parents, for other boys and girls. He eagerly awaits their prayers. What enormous power the prayer of children has. This becomes a model for grown-ups themselves: praying with simple and complete trust means praying as children pray.

As we look toward the future, how can we fail to think of the young? What is being held up to them? A society of "things" and not of "persons"? The right to do as they will from their earliest years, without any constraint?

We may well fear that tomorrow these same young people, once they have reached adulthood, will demand an explanation from their parents and their leaders for having deprived them of reasons for living because they failed to teach them the duties incumbent upon being endowed with intelligence and free will.

Christian families exist to form a communion of persons in love. As such, the Church and the family are each in its own way living representations in human history of the eternal loving communion of the three Persons of the Most Holy Trinity. In fact, the family is called the Church in miniature, "the domestic church," a particular expression of the Church through the human experience of love and common life. Like the Church, the family ought to be a place where the gospel is transmitted and from which the gospel radiates to other families and to the whole of society.

Catholic parents must learn to form their family as this domestic Church, a Church in the home where God is honored, His law is respected, prayer is a normal event, virtue is transmitted by word and example, and everyone shares the hopes, the problems, and sufferings of everyone else. All this is not to advocate a return to some outdated style of living; it is rather a return to the roots of human development and human happiness.

Jesus prays to His heavenly Father that all may be one; this prayer comes to His lips the day before His passion. But it is a prayer He already carries in Himself at the moment of His birth: "that they may all be one. As you, Father, are in me and I am in you, may they also be in us."

Was He not praying at that moment also for the unity of human families? He was certainly praying above all for the unity of the Church; but the family, sustained by a special sacrament, is the vital cell of the Church. So Jesus prayed from the very time of His coming into the world that all who believe in Him might give expression to their communion, starting with the profound unity of God's plan for conjugal love from which the family takes its origin.

We can therefore hold that Jesus prayed for the sacred and fundamental unity of every family. He prayed for the union of God's children in truth and charity. Having given the sincere gift of Himself in coming into this world, He prayed that all people, in founding a family, would become, for the good of that family, a sincere mutual gift of self: husbands and wives, parents and children, and all the generations that make up the family; every individual making their own particular contributions.

Christ's love is the source and the foundation of the love uniting spouses. It should be stressed that true conjugal love is what is meant here, and not mere spontaneous impulse. Today, sexuality is often exalted to the point of obscuring the profound nature of love. Certainly, sexual life, too, has its own genuine value, which can never be underestimated; but it is a limited value that is an insufficient basis for the marriage union, which by its nature depends on total personal commitment.

Every sound psychology and philosophy of love is in agreement on this point. Christian teaching also emphasizes the qualities of the individuals' unitive love and casts a higher light on it, raising it—by virtue of a sacrament—to the level of grace and of sharing in the divine love of Christ. Along these lines, St. Paul says of marriage, "This is a great mystery," in reference to Christ and the Church. For the Christian, this theological mystery is at the root of the ethics of marriage, conjugal love, and sexual life itself: "Husbands, love your wives, just as Christ loved the church and gave himself up for her."

Grace and the sacramental bond enable conjugal life, as a sign of and share in the love of Christ the Bridegroom, to be a way of holiness for Christian spouses and at the same time to be an effective incentive for the Church to invigorate the communion of the love that distinguishes her.

It is a fundamental duty of the Church to reaffirm strongly the doctrine of the indissolubility of marriage. To all those who in our times consider it too difficult or indeed impossible to be bound to one person for the whole of life, and to those caught up in a culture that rejects the indissolubility of marriage and openly mocks the commitment of spouses to fidelity, it is necessary to reconfirm the good news of the definitive nature of that conjugal love that has in Christ its foundation and strength.

Being rooted in the personal and total self-giving of the couple, and being required by the good of the children, the indissolubility of marriage finds its ultimate truth in the plan that God has manifested in His revelation: He wills and He communicates the indissolubility of marriage as a fruit, a sign, and a requirement of the absolutely faithful love that God has for humanity and that the Lord Jesus has for the Church.

The gift of the sacrament of Matrimony is at the same time a vocation and commandment for the Christian spouses that they may remain faithful to each other forever, beyond every trial and difficulty, in generous obedience to the holy will of the Lord: "Therefore what God has joined together, let no one separate."

To bear witness to the inestimable value of the indissolubility and fidelity of marriage is one of the most precious and most urgent tasks of Christian couples in our time. I praise and encourage those numerous couples who, though encountering no small difficulty, preserve and develop the value of indissolubility. Thus in a humble and courageous manner they perform the role committed to them

of being a sign—a small and precious sign, sometimes also subjected to temptation, but always
renewed—of the unfailing fidelity with which
God and Jesus Christ love each and every human
being.

By reason of their dignity and mission, Christian
parents also have the specific responsibility of educating their children in prayer, introducing them
to gradual discovery of the mystery of God and to
personal dialogue with Him. The concrete example
and living witness of parents is fundamental and
irreplaceable in educating their children to pray.
Only by praying together with their children can a
father and mother penetrate the innermost depths
of their children's hearts and leave an impression
that the future events in their lives will not be able
to efface.

Man and woman are called to live in the process
of cosmic creation, bringing with them the ability
to procreate in collaboration with God, who directly
creates the soul of each new human being. Through
mutual knowledge and love, and at the same time
through physical union, they will call to life beings
resembling themselves and, like them, created "in
the image of God." They will give life to their own
children, just as they received it from their parents.

This is the truth, both simple and great, about the family as it is presented in the pages of the book of Genesis and in the Gospels: in God's plan, marriage—indissoluble marriage—is the basis of a healthy and responsible family.

There is a creative act of God at every person's origin, a plan of love that awaits fulfillment. This fundamental truth, accessible even within the limited power of reason, permits one to catch a glimpse of the very mission inscribed in human sexuality: it is, in fact, called to cooperate with the creative power of God.

Conjugal love is the loftiest and most beautiful expression of human relations and self-giving, for it is essentially a desire for mutual growth. In this encounter based on reciprocal love, each is recognized for what they are and are called to express their personal talents and achieve their potential. The logic of the sincere gift of self is a source of joy, help, and understanding.

The bonds that unite a family are not only a matter of natural kinship or of shared life and experience. They are essentially holy and religious bonds. Marriage and the family are sacred realities. The sacredness of Christian marriage consists in the fact that in God's plan, the marriage covenant between a man and a woman becomes the image and symbol of the covenant that unites God and His People.

God's love is faithful and irrevocable, so those who have been married in Christ are called to remain faithful to each other forever. Remember, Jesus says to us: "Therefore what God has joined together, let no one separate." Contemporary society has a special need of the witness of couples who persevere in their union as an eloquent, even if sometimes suffering, sign in our human condition of the steadfastness of God's love. Day after day, Christian married couples are called to open their hearts ever more to the Holy Spirit, whose power never fails and who enables them to love each other as Christ has loved us.

As St. Paul writes to the Galatians, "The fruit of the Spirit is love, joy, peace, patience, kindness, generosity, faithfulness, gentleness, and self-control." All of this constitutes the rule of life and the program of personal development of Christian couples. And each Christian community has a great responsibility to sustain couples in their love.

From such love, Christian families are born. In them, children are welcomed as a splendid gift of God's goodness; and they are educated in the essential values of human life, learning above all that "man is more precious for what he is than for what he has."

Gender equality, as most women themselves point out, does not mean "sameness with men." This would only impoverish women and all of society by deforming or losing the unique richness and the inherent value of femininity. In the Church's outlook, women and men have been called by the Creator to live in profound communion with one another with reciprocal knowledge and giving of self, acting together for the common good with the complementary characteristics of that which is feminine and masculine.

Where communities or countries lack basic social infrastructures and economic opportunities, women and children are the first to experience marginalization. And yet where poverty abounds, or in the face of the devastation of conflict and war, or the tragedy of migration, forced or otherwise, it is very often women who maintain the vestiges of human dignity, defend the family, and preserve cultural and religious values. History is written almost exclusively as the narrative of men's achievements, when in fact its better part is most often molded by women's determined and persevering action for good.

The trivialization of sexuality, especially in the media, and the acceptance in some societies of a sexuality without moral restraint and without accountability, are deleterious to women, increasing the challenges that they face in sustaining their personal dignity and their service to life. In a society that follows this path, the temptation to use abortion as a so-called solution to the unwanted results of sexual promiscuity and irresponsibility is very strong. And here again, it is the woman who bears the heaviest burden: often left alone, or pressured into terminating the life of her child before it is born, she must then bear the burden of her conscience, which forever reminds her that she has taken the life of her child.

A radical solidarity with women requires that the underlying causes that make a child unwanted be addressed. There will never be justice—including equality, development, and peace—for women, or for men, unless there is an unfailing determination to respect, serve, love, and protect every human life, at every stage and in every situation.

No response to women's issues can ignore women's role in the family or take lightly the fact that every new life is entrusted to the protection and care of the woman carrying it in her womb. In order to respect this natural order of things, it is necessary to counter the misconception that the role of motherhood is oppressive to women and that a commitment to her family, particularly to her children, prevents a woman from reaching personal fulfillment and women as a whole from having an influence in society. It is a disservice not only to children, but also to women and society itself, when a woman is made to feel guilty for wanting to remain in the home, and nurture and care for her children.

A mother's presence in the family, so critical to the stability and growth of this basic unit of society, should instead be recognized, applauded, and supported in every possible way. By the same token, society needs to, and ought to, strive for a situation in which mothers will not be forced by economic circumstances to move away from the home in search of work.

Experience confirms that there must be a social reevaluation of the mother's role, of the toil connected with it, and of the need that children have for care, love, and affection in order that they may develop into responsible, morally and religiously mature, and psychologically stable persons. It will be to the credit of society to make it possible for a mother—without inhibiting her freedom, without psychological or practical discrimination, and without penalizing her as compared with other women—to devote herself to taking care of her children and educating them in accordance with their needs, which vary with age. Having to abandon these tasks in order to take up paid work outside the home is wrong from the point of view of the good of society and of the family when it contradicts or hinders these primary goals of the mission of a mother.

The true advancement of women requires that labor should be structured in such a way that women do not have to pay for their advancement by abandoning what is specific to them and at the expense of the family, in which women as mothers have an irreplaceable role.

Women also have the task of assuring the moral dimension of culture, the dimension—namely, of a culture worthy of the person—of an individual yet social life. "It is not good that the man should be alone; I will make him a helper as his partner." God entrusted the human being to woman. Certainly, every human being is entrusted to each and every other human being, but in a special way the human being is entrusted to woman precisely because the woman, in virtue of her special experience of motherhood, is seen to have a specific sensitivity toward the human person and all that constitutes the individual's true welfare, beginning with the fundamental value of life.

Older people are oftentimes unjustly considered as unproductive, if not directly an insupportable burden. I want to remind older people that the Church calls and expects them to continue to exercise their mission in the apostolic and missionary life. This is not only a possibility for them, but it is their duty in this time of their life when age itself provides opportunities in some specific and basic way.

The Bible delights in presenting the older person as the symbol of someone rich in wisdom and fear of the Lord. In this sense, the gift of older people can be specifically that of being witness to tradition in the faith, both in the Church and in society, the teacher of the lessons of life, and the worker of charity.

At this moment, the growing number of older people in different countries worldwide and the retirement of people from various professions and the workplace provides older people with a new opportunity in the apostolate. They must have a clear knowledge that their roles in the Church and society do not stop at a certain age. As the psalmist says: "In old age they still produce fruit; they are always green and full of sap, showing that the Lord is upright."

Older people, with health problems and the decline of their physical strength, are particularly associated with Christ in His passion and on the Cross. It is therefore possible to penetrate ever more deeply into this mystery of the redeeming sacrifice, and to give the witness of faith in this mystery, of the courage and hope that derive from it, in the various difficulties and trials of old age.

Finally, let us remember that each of us comes into the world within a family, and can be said to owe to the family the very fact of our existing as an individual. When we have no family, the person coming into the world develops an anguished sense of pain and loss, one that will subsequently burden their whole life.

The Church draws near with loving concern to all who experience situations such as these, for she knows well the fundamental role that the family is called upon to play. Furthermore, she knows that people go forth from their families in order to realize in new family units their particular vocations in life. Even if someone chooses to remain single, the family continues to be, as it were, an existential horizon, that fundamental community in which the whole network of social relations is grounded, from the closest and most immediate to the most distant.

Every effort should be made so that the family will be recognized as the primordial and, in a certain sense, sovereign society. The sovereignty of the family is essential for the good of society. A truly sovereign and spiritually vigorous nation is always made up of strong families who are aware of their vocation and mission in history.

Be bearers of peace and joy within the family. Grace elevates and perfects love, and, with it, grants us the indispensable family virtues of humility, the spirit of service and sacrifice, parental and filial affection, respect, and mutual understanding.

Happy is everyone who fears the Lord,
who walks in his ways.

Your wife will be like a fruitful vine
within your house;
your children will be like olive shoots
around your table.
Thus shall the man be blessed
who fears the Lord.

—PSALM 128:1, 3–4

LEAD US IN TRUTH!

Lead in truth, O Christ, the fathers and mothers
of families in the Church.
Urged on and strengthened by the sacramental
grace of marriage,
and aware of being on earth the visible sign of
your unfailing love for the Church.
Lead in truth, O Christ, the young people of the
Church.
Let them not be attracted by the new idols,
such as exaggerated consumerism, prosperity at
all costs,
moral permissiveness, protest expressed with
violence,
but rather let them live with the joy of your
message,
which is the message of the Beatitudes.
Lead in truth, O Christ, all the faithful of
the Church,
may we become before the world courageous
witnesses to Your mission of salvation,
happy to be sons and daughters of God—with
You and all humanity!
Lead us in truth, O Christ, always!
Amen.

—JOHN PAUL II

TEN

On Suffering

The sick, the elderly, the handicapped, and the dying teach us that weakness is a creative part of human living, and that suffering can be embraced with no loss of dignity. Without the presence of these people in our midst we might be tempted to think of health, strength, and power as the only important values to be pursued in life. But the wisdom of Christ and the power of Christ are to be seen in the weakness of those who share his sufferings.

—JOHN PAUL II

He said to me, "My grace is sufficient for you, for power is made perfect in weakness." So, I will boast all the more gladly of my weaknesses, so that the power of Christ may dwell in me.

—2 CORINTHIANS 12:9

*I*n the presence of so much suffering in our world, we cannot remain indifferent or passive. But before asking about the responsibility of others, we must listen first to the voice of the Divine Master. He urges us to imitate the Good Samaritan, who helped the man attacked by robbers on the road from Jerusalem to Jericho. The Samaritan spent his energy, time, and money helping the man—though, first and foremost, he offered him his compassionate heart. Christians know we are called to put Christ's teaching into practice: "Just as you did it to one of the least of these who are members of my family, you did it to me."

In the parable of the Good Samaritan, Jesus teaches us to show a generous initiative on behalf of those who are suffering. He reveals His presence in all who are in need and pain, so that every act of helping the suffering is done to Christ Himself. This means that suffering, intended to sanctify those who suffer, is also meant to sanctify those who help and comfort them.

The reality of suffering is ever before our eyes and often in the body, soul, and heart of each of us. Pain has always been a great riddle of human existence. However, ever since Jesus redeemed the world by His passion and death, a new perspective has been opened: through suffering, one can grow in self-giving and attain the highest degree of love because of Him who "loved us and gave himself up for us." As a sharing in the mystery of the Cross, suffering can now be accepted and lived as a cooperation in Christ's saving mission.

In the Cross, the "Gospel of suffering" has been revealed to Christians. Jesus recognized in His sacrifice the way established by the Father for the redemption of humanity, and He followed this way.

He also told His disciples that they would be associated with this sacrifice: "Very truly, I tell you, you will weep and mourn, but the world will rejoice."

This prediction, however, is not the only one, nor is it the final word because it is completed by the announcement that their pain will be changed into joy: "You will have pain, but your pain will turn into joy." Christ's passion is oriented toward the Resurrection. Human beings are thus associated with the mystery of the Cross in order to share joyfully in the mystery of the Resurrection.

For this reason, Jesus did not hesitate to proclaim the blessedness of those who suffer: "Blessed are those who mourn, for they will be comforted. Blessed are those who are persecuted for righteousness' sake, for theirs is the kingdom of heaven. Blessed are you when people revile you and persecute you and utter all kinds of evil against you falsely on my account. Rejoice and be glad, for your reward is great in heaven."

This blessedness can only be understood if one admits that human life is not limited to our time spent on earth, but is wholly directed to perfect joy and fullness of life in the hereafter. Earthly suffering, when accepted in love, is like a bitter kernel containing the seed of new life, the treasure of divine glory to be given humanity in eternity.

Although the sight of a world burdened with evil and misfortune of every sort is often so wretched, nevertheless the hope of a better world of love and grace is hidden within it. It is this hope that is nourished by Christ's promise.

A basic principle of the Christian faith is the fruitfulness of suffering and, hence, the call of all who suffer to unite themselves with Christ's redemptive sacrifice. Suffering thus becomes an offering, an oblation; this has happened and still does in so many holy souls. With this support, those who suffer, united in faith with Jesus, experience in this life a joy that can seem humanly unexplainable.

Especially those who are oppressed by apparently senseless moral suffering find in Jesus' moral suffering the meaning of their own trials, and go with Him into the Garden at Gethsemane. In Him they find the strength to accept pain with holy abandon and trusting obedience to the Father's will. And they feel rising from within their hearts the prayer of Gethsemane: "Yet, not my will but yours be done."

In Christ they also find the courage to offer their pain for the salvation of all, having learned the mysterious fruitfulness of every sacrifice from the offering on Calvary, according to the principle set forth by Jesus: "Very truly, I tell you, unless a grain of wheat falls into the earth and dies, it remains just a single grain; but if it dies, it bears much fruit."

Jesus' teaching is confirmed by the Apostle Paul, who had a very vivid awareness of sharing in Christ's passion in his own life and of the cooperation he could thus offer for the good of the Christian community. Because of union with Christ in suffering, Paul could speak of completing within himself what was lacking, through the sufferings of Christ, for the sake of His Body, the Church. Convinced of the fruitfulness of his union with the redeeming Passion, he stated: "So death is at work in us, but life in you."

Whoever follows Christ, whoever accepts St. Paul's theology of pain, knows that a precious grace, a divine favor, is connected with suffering, even if it is a grace that remains a mystery to us because it is hidden under the appearances of a painful destiny. It is certainly not easy to discover in suffering the genuine divine love that wishes, through the acceptance of suffering, to raise human life to the level of Christ's saving love. Faith, however, enables us to cling to this mystery and, despite everything, brings peace and joy to the soul of the

one suffering; at times he even says with St. Paul:
"I am filled with consolation; I am overjoyed in all
our affliction."

Whoever relives the spirit of Christ's sacrifice is
moved to imitate Him by helping others who are
suffering. Jesus relieved countless human sufferings
around Him. In this respect, too, He is a perfect
model. And He prescribed the command of mutual
love that implies compassion and reciprocal aid.

When so many of our brothers and sisters are
suffering, we cannot remain indifferent. Their dis-
tress must appeal to our conscience, the inner sanctuary where we come face to face with ourselves
and with God.

I would like to call our attention to the poverty
in our world, especially when it becomes destitu-
tion. There are millions of men, women, and children suffering every day from hunger, insecurity,
and marginalization. These situations constitute a
grave affront to human dignity and contribute to
social instability.

Poverty is driving masses of people to the edges
of society, or even worse, to extinction. For many
people, war has become a harsh everyday reality.
Societies interested only in material and ephemeral

goods are tending to marginalize those who are not useful to its purposes.

Faced with situations like these, involving real human tragedies, some prefer simply to close their eyes, taking refuge in indifference. Theirs is the attitude of Cain: "Am I my brother's keeper?" But we have the duty to remind everyone of God's severe admonishment: "What have you done? Listen; your brother's blood is crying out to me from the ground!"

The crowds of starving people—children, women, the elderly, immigrants, refugees, the unemployed—raise their cry of suffering. They implore us, hoping to be heard. How can we not open our ears and our hearts and start to make available those loaves and fishes that God has put into our hands?

If each one of us contributes, we can all do something for them. Of course, this will require sacrifice, which calls for a deep inner conversion. Certainly, it will involve changing our exaggerated consumerist behavior, combating hedonism, and resisting attitudes of indifference and the tendency to disregard our personal responsibilities.

With more than 800 million people suffering from malnutrition, it is often difficult to find immediate solutions for improving these tragic situations. We must nevertheless seek them together so that we will no longer have, side by side, the starving and the wealthy, the very poor and the very rich, those who lack the necessary means and others who lavishly waste them. Such contrasts between poverty and wealth are intolerable for humanity.

It is from the love of God that Christians learn to help the needy and to share with them their own material and spiritual goods. Such concern not only provides those experiencing hardship with material help, but also represents an opportunity for the spiritual growth of the giver. But there is a higher motivation that Christ indicated to us by His own example when He said: "The Son of Man has nowhere to lay his head."

By these words, the Lord wished to show His total openness to His heavenly Father, whose will He was determined to carry out without letting Himself be hindered by the possession of worldly goods. For there is always a danger that earthly realities will take the place of God in the human heart. As Christians, we must direct our entire lives to Him, for we know that in this world we have no fixed abode: "But our citizenship is in heaven."

Ensuring a suitable habitat for everyone is demanded by the respect owed to every human being and, therefore, is a measure of civilization and the condition for a peaceful, fraternal society. By virtue of our human dignity, every person must be guaranteed a lodging that offers not only physical shelter, but also a suitable place for satisfying their social, cultural, and spiritual needs.

If states have precise duties in providing housing, much also depends on the sensitivity of private individuals. Moreover, how can political guidelines inspired by justice and solidarity be promoted if these values are not woven into the fabric of a society as a whole? I hope that everyone—particularly those who believe in the gospel of Christ—will develop a greater sensitivity to the concrete, urgent issue of the right to housing.

For each of us, moderation and simplicity ought to become the criteria of our daily lives. The quantity of goods consumed by a tiny fraction of the world population produces a demand greater than available resources. A reduction of this demand constitutes a first step in alleviating poverty, provided that it is accompanied by effective measures to guarantee a fair distribution of the world's wealth.

In this regard, the Gospel invites believers not
to accumulate the goods of this passing world: "Do
not store up for yourselves treasures on earth, where
moth and rust consume and where thieves break in
and steal; but store up for yourselves treasures in
heaven." This is a duty intrinsic to the Christian
vocation, no less than the duty of working to overcome poverty. A person who is concerned solely or
primarily with possessing and enjoying, who is no
longer able to control their instincts and passions,
or to subordinate them in obedience to the truth,
cannot be free. Obedience to the truth about God
and humankind is the first condition of freedom,
making it possible for a person to order their needs
and desires, and to choose the means of satisfying
them according to a correct scale of values.

It is necessary once more to state the characteristic
principle of Christian social doctrine: the goods of
this world are originally meant for all. The right to
private property is valid and necessary, but it does
not nullify the value of this principle.

As far as the Church is concerned, the social
message of the Gospel must not be considered
a theory, but above all else a basis and a motivation for action. Inspired by this message, some of
the first Christians distributed their goods to the

poor, bearing witness to the fact that, despite different social origins, it was possible for people to live together in peace and harmony. Through the power of God, down through the centuries, monks tilled the land; religious men and women founded hospitals and shelters for the poor; confraternities as well as individual men and women of all states of life devoted to Jesus came to proclaim the Gospel to the poor, to those who, aware of their limitations, felt the need of help from on high. For believers, this is both an individual and a social duty.

Distinguishing between the necessary and the dispensable enables each of us to be more open and more generous to our needy brothers and sisters, to purify our personal relationship with money, and to moderate our attachment to the goods of this world.

Even if we do not have at our disposal riches and concrete capacities to meet the needs of our neighbor, we can at least open our hearts to their necessities and relieve them of their suffering as far as possible. Remember the widow's mite; she threw into the treasury of the temple only two small coins, but with them all her great love: "But she out of her poverty has put in everything she had, all she had to live on."

Above all, it is the interior value of our giving that counts: the readiness to share everything, the readiness to give oneself. St. Paul wrote: "If I give away all my possessions, . . . but do not have love, I gain nothing." St. Augustine also writes: "If you stretch out your hand to give, but have not mercy in your heart, you have not done anything; but if you have mercy in your heart, even when you have nothing to give with your hand, God accepts your alms."

Our heartfelt charity restores hope and healing to the poor and suffering, who realize they are truly loved by God. In all of us, all the people of good-will, we must foster this awareness of the need to cooperate in meeting the challenge of sharing, of the equitable distribution of goods, and of joining forces. In this way, everyone will contribute to the building up of a more just and fraternal society—based on love—because love is a witness of the Kingdom to come, and it alone can radically transform the world.

And our charity goes beyond justice, for it is an invitation to go beyond the order of mere equity to the order of love and self-giving. Sometimes, action in communion is more eloquent than any teaching; and actions joined to words give particularly effective witness. The disciples of the Lord will recall that serving the poor and suffering is serving Christ, who is the light of the world. By living daily in the love that comes from Him, the faithful help spread light in the world.

And finally, I ask of you all, become friends to those who have no friends. Become family to those who have no family. And become community to those who have no community.

Is not this the fast that I choose:
    to loose the bonds of injustice,
        to undo the thongs of the yoke,
to let the oppressed go free,
    and to break every yoke?
Is it not to share your bread with the hungry,
    and bring the homeless poor into your house;
when you see the naked, to cover them,
    and not to hide yourself from your own kin?

                                    —Isaiah 58:6–7

LET THOSE WHO HAVE . . .
Let those who have a superabundance
avoid shutting themselves up in themselves,
avoid attachment to their own wealth,
avoid spiritual blindness.
Let them avoid all this with all their strength.
May the truth of the Gospel contained in these
    words accompany them always:
"Blessed are the poor in spirit, for theirs is the
    kingdom of heaven."
May this truth make them uneasy.
May it be a continual warning and a challenge for
    them.
May it not allow them even for a minute to
    become blind
out of the selfishness and the satisfaction of their
    own desires.
Amen.

—JOHN PAUL II

ELEVEN

On Christian Vocation and Working in the World

Let us listen to the words of our Lord Jesus Christ, who says: "Look around you, and see how the fields are ripe for harvesting. The reaper is already receiving wages and is gathering fruit for eternal life, so that sower and reaper may rejoice together." And let us ask—let us ask Him with our whole soul for this reaping. And looking at "the fields . . . ripe for harvesting," let us think that harvesters are needed just as sowers were first needed. And let us say to Christ who redeemed us with His blood: Lord, here I am! Take me as sower and as reaper in Your kingdom. Lord, here I am! Send laborers to the harvest. "Send out laborers into his harvest."

—JOHN PAUL II

You are the salt of the earth; but if salt has lost its taste, how can its saltiness be restored? It is no longer good for anything, but is thrown out and trampled under foot. You are the light of the world. A city built on a hill cannot be hid. No one after lighting a lamp puts it under the bushel basket, but on the lampstand, and it gives light to all in the house. In the same way, let your light shine before others, so that they may see your good works and give glory to your Father in heaven.

—MATTHEW 5:13–16

*G*od calls me and sends me forth as a laborer in His vineyard. He calls me and sends me forth to work for the coming of His Kingdom in history. This personal vocation and mission defines the dignity and the responsibility of each member of the faithful. It makes up the focal point of the whole work of spiritual formation, the purpose of which is the joyous and grateful recognition of this dignity and the faithful and generous living out of this responsibility.

In fact, from eternity God has thought of us and has loved us as unique individuals. Every one of us He called by name, as the Good Shepherd "calls his own sheep by name." However, only in the unfolding of the history of our lives and its events is the eternal plan of God revealed to each of us. Therefore, it is a gradual process; in a certain sense, one that happens day by day.

To be able to discover the actual will of the Lord in our lives always involves the following: a receptive listening to the Word of God and the Church, fervent and constant prayer, recourse to wise and loving spiritual guides, and a faithful discernment of the gifts and talents given by God. In the life of each member of the faithful, there are particularly significant and decisive moments for discerning God's call and embracing the mission entrusted by Him. No one must forget that the Lord, as the Master of the laborers in the vineyard, calls us at every hour of our lives so as to make His holy will more precisely and explicitly known. Therefore, the fundamental and continuous attitude of the disciple should be one of vigilance and a conscious attentiveness to the voice of God.

It is not a question of simply *knowing* what God wants from each of us in the various situations of life. The individual must *do* what God wants, as we are reminded in the words that Mary, the Mother of Jesus, addressed to the servants at Cana: "Do whatever he tells you." This, then, is the marvelous yet demanding task awaiting all Christians at every moment: to grow always in the knowledge of the richness of Baptism and faith, as well as to live it more fully.

Each Christian vocation comes from God and is God's gift. However, it is never bestowed outside of or independent of the Church. Instead, it always comes about in the Church because, as the Second Vatican Council reminds us, "God has willed to make men holy and save them, not as individuals without any bond or link between them, but rather to make them into a people who might acknowledge Him and serve Him in holiness." Christian vocation, whatever shape it takes, is a gift whose purpose is to build up the Church and to increase the Kingdom of God in the world.

In discovering and living our proper vocation and mission, we must be formed according to the union that exists from our being members of the Church and citizens of human society.

There cannot be two parallel lives in our existence: on the one hand, the so-called spiritual life,
with its values and demands; and on the other,
the so-called secular life, that is, life in a family,
at work, in social relationships, in the responsibilities of public life, and in culture. The branch,
engrafted to the vine that is Christ, bears its fruit
in every sphere of existence and activity. In fact,
every area of our lives, as different as they are,
enters into the plan of God, who desires that these
very areas be the places in time where the love of
Christ is revealed and realized for both the glory
of the Father and service of others.

Every activity, every situation, every precise
responsibility—as, for example, skill and solidarity in
work, love and dedication in the family and the education of children, service to society and public life,
and the promotion of truth in the area of culture—
all these are the occasions ordained by Providence.

The Word of God's revelation is profoundly
marked by the fundamental truth that humanity,
created in the image of God, shares by their work
in the activity of the Creator; and that humanity
continues to develop that activity, and perfects it
as they advance further in the discovery of the

resources and values contained in the whole of creation. We find this truth at the very beginning of Sacred Scripture, in the book of Genesis, where the creation activity itself is presented in the form of "work" done by God during "six days"—"resting" on the seventh day.

Genesis concludes the description of each day of creation with the statement: "And God saw that it was good." This description of creation is also the first "gospel of work," for it shows what the dignity of work consists of: it teaches that humanity ought to imitate God, our Creator, in working because we alone have the unique characteristic of likeness to God. Therefore, we ought to imitate God in working, and also in resting, since God Himself wished to present His own creative activity under the form of work and rest.

The truth that by means of work humanity participates in the activity of God Himself, his Creator, was given particular prominence by Jesus Christ—the Jesus at whom many of His first listeners in Nazareth were astonished, saying, "Where did this man get all this? What is this wisdom that has been given to him? What deeds of power are being done by his hands! Is not this the carpenter?" For

Jesus not only proclaimed but first and foremost fulfilled by His deeds the Gospel—the Word of eternal Wisdom—that had been entrusted to Him. Therefore, this was also "the Gospel of work" because He who proclaimed it was Himself a man of work, a craftsman like Joseph of Nazareth.

Even if we do not find in His words a special command to work, nevertheless, the eloquence of the life of Christ is unequivocal: He belongs to the working world; He has appreciation and respect for human work. It can indeed be said that He looks with love upon human work and the different forms that it takes, seeing in each one of these forms a particular facet of humanity's likeness with God, the Creator and Father.

All work, whether manual or intellectual, is inevitably linked with toil. The book of Genesis expresses it in a truly penetrating manner: the original blessing of work contained in the very mystery of creation and connected with humanity's elevation as the image of God is contrasted with the curse that sin brought with it: "cursed is the ground because of you; in toil you shall eat of it all the days of your life."

Sweat and toil, which work necessarily involves, present the Christian and everyone who is called to follow Christ with the possibility of sharing lovingly in the work that Christ came to do. This work of salvation came about through suffering and death on a Cross. By enduring the toil of work in union with Christ crucified for us, humanity collaborates with the Son of God for the redemption of itself. We show ourselves as true disciples of Christ by carrying the Cross in our turn every day in the activity that we are called upon to perform. The Christian finds in human work a small part of the Cross of Christ and accepts it in the same spirit of redemption in which Christ accepted His Cross for us.

The right to work must be combined with that of freedom to choose one's own activity. These prerogatives, however, must not be understood in an individualistic sense, but in relation to the vocation to service and cooperation with others. Freedom is not exercised morally without considering its relationship and reciprocity with other freedoms. These should be understood not so much as restrictions, but as conditions for the development of individual freedom and as an exercise of the duty to contribute to the growth of society as a whole.

Thus, work is primarily a right because it is a duty arising from humanity's social relations. It expresses humanity's vocation to service and solidarity.

A charity that loves and serves the person can never be separated from justice. Each in its own way demands the full, effective acknowledgment of the rights of the individual to which society is ordered in all its structures and institutions.

In order to achieve their task directed to the Christian animation of the temporal order, in the sense of serving persons and society, the faithful are never to relinquish their participation in public life; that is, in the many different economic, social, legislative, administrative, and cultural areas which are intended to promote the common good. Every person has a right and duty to participate in public life, albeit in a diversity and complementarity of forms, levels, tasks, and responsibilities. Charges of careerism, idolatry of power, egoism, and corruption that are oftentimes directed at persons in government, parliaments, the ruling classes, or political parties—as well as the common opinion that participating in politics is an absolute moral danger—do not in the least justify either skepticism or an absence on the part of Christians in public life.

The spirit of service is a fundamental element in the exercise of political power. This spirit of service, together with the necessary competence and efficiency, can make virtuous the activity of persons in public life, which is justly demanded by the rest of the people. To accomplish this requires a full-scale battle and a determination to overcome every temptation, such as: the recourse to disloyalty and to falsehood; the waste of public funds for the advantage of a few and those with special interests; and the use of ambiguous and illicit means for acquiring, maintaining, and increasing power at any cost.

We must bear witness to those human and Gospel values that are intimately connected with political activity itself, such as liberty and justice, solidarity, faithful and unselfish dedication for the good of all, a simple lifestyle, and a preferential love for the poor and the least. This demands that we always be animated by a real participation in the life of the Church and enlightened by her social doctrine.

When people think that they possess the secret of a perfect social organization which makes evil impossible, they also think that they can use any means, including violence and deceit, in order to bring that organization into being. Politics then becomes a secular religion that operates under the illusion of creating paradise in this world; but no political society—which possesses its own autonomy and laws—can ever be confused with the Kingdom of God.

The Gospel parable of the weeds among the wheat teaches us that it is for God alone to separate the subjects of the Kingdom from the subjects of the Evil One, and that this judgment will take place at the end of time. By presuming to anticipate judgment here and now, people put themselves in the place of God and set themselves against the patience of God.

Through Christ's sacrifice on the Cross, the victory of the Kingdom of God has been achieved once and for all. Nevertheless, the Christian life involves a struggle against temptation and the forces of evil. Only at the end of history will the Lord return in glory for the final judgment with the establishment of a new heaven and a new earth. But as long as time lasts, the struggle between good and evil continues even in the human heart itself.

Nowadays there is a tendency to claim that agnosticism and skeptical relativism are the philosophies and the basic attitudes that correspond to democratic forms of political life. Those who are convinced that they know the truth and firmly adhere to it are considered unreliable from a democratic point of view, since they do not accept that truth is determined by the majority or that it is subject to variation according to different political trends.

But it must be observed in this regard that if there is no ultimate truth to guide and direct political activity, then ideas and convictions can easily be manipulated for reasons of power. As history demonstrates, a democracy without values easily turns into open or thinly disguised totalitarianism.

In the context of the transformations taking place in the world of economy and work, we have the responsibility of being in the forefront in working out a solution to the very serious problems of: growing unemployment; overcoming numerous injustices that come from organizations of work which lack a proper goal; making the workplace become a community of persons respected in their uniqueness and in their right to participation; developing new solidarity among those who participate in a common work; raising up new forms of business enterprise; and looking again at systems of commerce, finance, and exchange of technology. To such an end, we must accomplish our work with professional competence, with human honesty, with a Christian spirit. When a firm makes a profit, this means that production factors have been properly employed and corresponding human needs have been duly satisfied.

But profitability is not the only indicator of a firm's condition. It is possible for the financial

accounts to be in order, and yet for the people—
who make up the firm's most valuable asset—to be
humiliated and their dignity offended.

Besides being morally inadmissible, this will
eventually have negative repercussions on the
firm's economic efficiency. In fact, the purpose of
a business firm is not simply to make a profit, but
is to be found in its very existence as a community
of persons who in various ways are endeavoring to
satisfy their basic needs, and who form a particular
group at the service of the whole of society. Profit
is a regulator of the life of a business, but it is not
the only one. Other human and moral factors must
also be considered that, in the long term, are at
least equally important for the life of a business.

There are collective and qualitative needs that
cannot be satisfied by market mechanisms. There
are important human needs that escape its logic.
There are goods that by their very nature cannot
and must not be bought or sold.

Certainly the mechanisms of the market offer
secure advantages: they help to utilize resources
better; they promote the exchange of products;
above all, they give central place to the person's
desires and preferences, which, in a contract, meet
the desires and preferences of another person.

Nevertheless, these mechanisms carry the risk of an idolatry of the market.

The Church calls upon each of us to be present as signs of courage and intellectual creativity in the privileged places of culture, that is, the world of education—school and university—places of scientific and technological research, and the areas of artistic creativity and work in the humanities. Such a presence is intended not only for the recognition and possible purification of the elements that critically burden existing culture, but also for the elevation of these cultures through the riches that have their source in the Gospel and the Christian faith.

Christian wisdom, which the Church teaches by divine authority, continuously inspires the faithful of Christ zealously to endeavor to relate human affairs and activities with religious values in a single living synthesis. Under the direction of these values, all things are mutually connected for the glory of God and the integral development of the human person, a development that includes both corporal and spiritual well-being.

Indeed, the Church's mission of spreading the Gospel not only demands that the Good News be

preached ever more widely and to ever greater num-
bers of men and women, but that the very power
of the Gospel should permeate thought patterns,
standards of judgment, and norms of behavior. In
a word, it is necessary that the whole of human culture be steeped in the Gospel.

The cultural atmosphere in which human beings
live has a great influence upon their way of thinking
and, thus, of acting. Therefore, a division between
faith and culture is more than a small impediment
to evangelization, while a culture penetrated with
the Christian spirit is an instrument that favors the
spreading of the Good News.

The figure of St. Joseph recalls the urgent need to
give a soul to the world of work. His life, marked
by listening to God and by familiarity with Christ,
appears as a harmonious synthesis of faith and life,
of personal fulfillment and love for one's brothers
and sisters, of daily commitment, and of trust in
the future.

May his witness remind those who work that
only by accepting the primacy of God and the light
that comes from Christ's Cross and Resurrection
can they fulfill the conditions of a labor worthy of
humanity—and find in daily toil a glimmer of new

life, of the new good, as if it were an announcement of "new heavens and a new earth" in which
humanity and the world participate precisely
through the toil that goes with work.

Let the favor of the Lord our God be upon us,
and prosper for us the work of our hands—
O prosper the work of our hands!

                       —Psalm 90:17

FOR THE WORKERS

I pray to God ardently for the happiness of all:
that your just aspirations may be realized;
that the moments and the reasons of crisis may be
    overcome;
that work will never be an alienation
    for anyone;
that, on the contrary, it may be honored by
    everyone as it deserves,
so that justice and even more love may
    triumph in it;
that the environment of work will really be fit for
    humanity,
and that humanity may be able to appreciate it as
    an extension of their own family;
that work may help men and women to be more
    truly who they are;
and that, with the commitment of everyone,
it may be possible to arrive at the construction of
    a new society and a new world,
in the full realization of justice, freedom,
    and peace.
Amen.

—JOHN PAUL II

TWELVE

On God the Father

In the name of Jesus Christ crucified and risen, in the spirit of His messianic mission, enduring in the history of humanity, we raise our voices and pray that the Love which is in the Father may once again be revealed at this stage in history, and that, through the work of the Son and the Holy Spirit, it may be shown to be present in our modern world and to be more powerful than sin and death.

—JOHN PAUL II

For this reason I bow my knees before the Father, from whom every family in heaven and on earth takes its name. I pray that, according to the riches of his glory, he may grant that you may be strengthened in your inner being with power through his Spirit, and that Christ may dwell in your hearts through faith.

—EPHESIANS 3:14–17

The whole of the Christian life is like a great pilgrimage to the house of the Father, whose unconditional love for every human creature, and in particular for the "prodigal son," we discover anew each day. This pilgrimage takes place in the heart of each person, extends to the believing community, and then reaches to the whole of humanity.

The recent Jubilee, centered on the person of Christ, became a great act of praise to the Father: "Blessed be the God and Father of our Lord Jesus

Christ, who has blessed us in Christ with every spiritual blessing in the heavenly places, just as he chose us in Christ before the foundation of the world to be holy and blameless before him in love."

The Church, as a reconciled and reconciling community, cannot forget that at the source of her gift and mission is the initiative, full of compassionate love and mercy, of our God, who is love and who, out of love, created human beings. He created us so that we might live in friendship with Him and in communion with one another.

God is faithful to His eternal plan even when humanity, under the impulse of the Evil One and carried away by our own pride, abuses the freedom given to us that we may love and generously seek what is good, and instead refuses to obey our Lord and Father. God is faithful even when humanity, instead of responding with love to God's love, opposes Him and treats Him like a rival, deluding ourselves and relying on our own power, with the resulting break of relationship with the One who created us. In spite of this transgression on our part, God remains faithful in love.

It is certainly true that the story of the Garden of Eden makes us think about the tragic consequences of rejecting the Father, which becomes evident in humanity's inner disorder and in the breakdown of harmony between man and woman, brother and brother. Refusal of God's fatherly love and of His loving gifts is always at the root of humanity's divisions.

But we know that God, "rich in mercy" like the father in the parable of the Prodigal Son, does not close His heart to any of His children. He waits for us, looks for us, and goes to meet us at the place where the refusal of communion imprisons us in isolation and division. He calls us to gather about His table in the joy of the feast of forgiveness and reconciliation. This initiative on God's part is made concrete and manifest in the redemptive act of Christ, which radiates through the world by means of the ministry of the Church.

Revelation and faith teach us not only to meditate in the abstract upon the mystery of God as the "Father of mercies," but also to have recourse to that mercy in the name of Christ and in union with Him. Did not Christ say that our Father, who "sees in secret," is always waiting for us to have recourse to Him in every need and always waiting for us to study His mystery—the mystery of the Father and His love?

Although God "dwells in unapproachable light," He speaks to humanity by means of the whole of the universe: "Ever since the creation of the world his eternal power and divine nature, invisible though they are, have been understood and seen through the things he has made." This indirect and imperfect knowledge, achieved by the intellect seeking God by means of creatures through the visible world, nevertheless falls short of a vision of the Father. "No one has ever seen God," writes St. John, in order to stress the truth that "the only Son, who is close to the Father's heart, who has made him known."

This "making known" of the Father by Christ reveals God in the most profound mystery of His being—the Trinity, the one and three—surrounded by "unapproachable light." Through this "making known" by Christ, we know God above all in His relationship of love for humanity. It is precisely here that "his eternal power and divine nature, invisible though they are" becomes in a special way "visible," incomparably more visible than through all the other "things he has made." It becomes visible in Christ and through Christ, through His actions and His words, and finally through His death on the Cross and His Resurrection.

God created man and woman in His own image and likeness: calling them to existence through love and, at the same time, for love. God is love and in Himself He lives a mystery of personal loving communion. Creating the human race in His own image and continually keeping it in being, God inscribed in the humanity of man and woman the vocation, and thus the capacity and responsibility, of love and communion. Love is therefore the fundamental and innate vocation of every human being.

The vocation to love, understood as true openness to our fellow human beings and solidarity with them, is the most basic of all vocations. It is the origin of all vocations in life. That is what Jesus was looking for in the young man when He said, "Keep the commandments."

In other words: Serve God and your neighbor according to all the demands of a true and upright heart. And when the young man indicated that he was already following that path, Jesus invited him to an even greater love: Leave all and come, follow Me; leave everything that concerns only yourself and join Me in the immense task of saving the world. Along the path of each person's existence, the Lord has something for each one to do.

Jesus asks us to follow Him and to imitate Him along the path of love, a love that gives itself completely to others out of love for God: "This is my commandment, that you love one another as I have loved you." The word *as* requires imitation of Jesus and of His love, of which the washing of feet is a sign: "So if I, your Lord and Teacher, have washed your feet, you also ought to wash one another's feet. For I have set you an example, that you also should do as I have done to you."

Jesus' way of acting and His words, His deeds, and His precepts constitute the moral rule of Christian life. Indeed, His actions, and in particular His passion and death on the Cross, are the living revelation of His love for the Father and for others. This is exactly the love that Jesus wishes to be imitated by all who follow Him. It is the "new" commandment: "I give you a new commandment, that you love one another. Just as I have loved you, you also should love one another. By this everyone will know that you are my disciples, if you have love for one another."

To imitate and live out the love of Christ is not possible for us by our own strength alone. We become capable of this love only by virtue of a gift received. As the Lord Jesus receives the love of His Father, so He in turn freely communicates that love to His disciples: "As the Father has loved me, so I have loved you; abide in my love." Christ's gift is His Spirit, whose first "fruit" is charity: "God's love has been poured into our hearts through the Holy Spirit that has been given to us."

St. Augustine asks, "Does love bring about the keeping of the commandments or does the keeping of the commandments bring about love?" And he answers, "But who can doubt that love comes first? For the one who does not love has no reason for keeping the commandments."

Love and life according to the Gospel cannot be thought of first and foremost as a kind of precept because what they demand is beyond our abilities. They are possible only as the result of a gift of God, who heals, restores, and transforms the human heart by His grace: "The law indeed was given through Moses; grace and truth came through Jesus Christ."

Humanity is called to a fullness of life that far exceeds the dimensions of our earthly existence because it consists in sharing the very life of God. The loftiness of this supernatural vocation reveals

the greatness and the inestimable value of human
life even in its temporal phase.

The Church knows that this Gospel of life,
which she has received from her Lord, has a profound and persuasive echo in the heart of every
person—believer and nonbeliever alike—because
it marvelously fulfills all the heart's expectations while infinitely surpassing them. Even in
the midst of difficulties and uncertainties, every
person sincerely open to truth and goodness
can, by the light of reason and the hidden action
of grace, come to recognize in the natural law,
written in the heart, the sacred value of human
life from its very beginning until its end, and
can affirm the right of every human being to
have this primary good respected to the highest
degree. Upon the recognition of this right, every
human community and the political community
itself are founded.

Humanity's life comes from God; it is His gift,
His image and imprint, a sharing in His breath
of life. God, therefore, is the sole Lord of this
life. God Himself makes this clear to Noah after
the Flood: "For your own lifeblood I will surely
require a reckoning: . . . each one for the blood of
another, I will require a reckoning for human life."
The biblical text is concerned to emphasize how

the sacredness of life has its foundation in God and in His creative activity: "So God created humankind in his image."

Human life and death are thus in the hands of God, in his power: "In his hand is the life of every living thing and the breath of every human being," exclaims Job. "The Lord kills and brings to life; he brings down to Sheol and raises up." He alone can say: "It is I who bring both death and life."

Precisely because of their faith, believers are called—as individuals and as a body—to be messengers and artisans of peace. Like others and even more than others, they are called to seek with humility and perseverance appropriate responses to the yearnings for security and freedom, solidarity and sharing, which are common to everyone in this world. A commitment to peace of course concerns every person of goodwill. Yet this is a duty that is especially incumbent upon all who profess faith in God and even more so upon Christians, who have as their guide and master the "Prince of Peace."

"Peace I leave with you; my peace I give to you," Christ has said to us. This divine promise fills us with the hope that peace is possible because nothing is impossible with God. For true peace is always

God's gift, and for us Christians it is a precious gift of the Risen Lord.

Peace is a fundamental good that involves respecting and promoting essential human values: the right to life at every stage of its development; the right to be respected, regardless of race, sex, or religious convictions; the right to the material goods necessary for life; the right to work and to a fair distribution of its fruits for a well-ordered and harmonious coexistence. As individuals, as believers, and even more as Christians, we must feel the commitment to living these values of justice, which are crowned by the supreme law of love: "You shall love your neighbor as yourself."

Peace is not a utopia, nor an inaccessible ideal, nor an unrealizable dream.

War is not an inevitable calamity.

Peace is possible.

And because it is possible, peace is our duty: our grave duty, our supreme responsibility.

Certainly peace is difficult; certainly it demands much goodwill, wisdom, and tenacity. But humanity can and must make the force of reason prevail over the reasons of force. And since peace, entrusted to the responsibility of men and women, remains even then a gift of God, it must also express itself in our prayer to Him who holds the destinies of all peoples in His hands.

For we ourselves were once foolish, disobedient, led astray, slaves to various passions and pleasures, passing our days in malice and envy, despicable, hating one another. But when the goodness and loving kindness of God our Savior appeared, he saved us, not because of any works of righteousness that we had done, but according to his mercy, through the water of rebirth and renewal by the Holy Spirit. This Spirit he poured out on us richly through Jesus Christ our Savior, so that, having been justified by his grace, we might become heirs according to the hope of eternal life.

— TITUS 3:3–7

O GOD, YOU ARE OUR CREATOR;
You are good and Your mercy knows no bounds.
To You arises the praise of every creature.
O God, You have given us an inner law by which
    we must live.
To do Your will is our task.
To follow Your ways is to know peace of heart.
To You we offer our homage.
Guide us on all the paths we travel upon
    this earth.
Free us from all the evil tendencies that lead our
    hearts away from Your will.
Never allow us to stray from You.
O God, judge of all humankind, help us to be
    included among
Your chosen ones on the last day.
O God, Author of peace and justice, give us true
    joy and authentic love,
and a lasting solidarity among peoples.
Give us Your everlasting gifts.
May the God of mercy, the God of love, and the
    God of peace
bless each of you and all the members of your
    families.
Amen.

                              —JOHN PAUL II

A Final Blessing

I leave you now with this prayer:
that the Lord Jesus will reveal Himself to each
one of you,
that He will give you the strength to go out and
profess that you are Christian,
that He will show you that He alone can fill your
hearts.
Accept His freedom and embrace His truth,
and be messengers of the certainty that you have
been truly liberated
through the death and resurrection of the Lord
Jesus.
This will be the new experience, the powerful
experience,
that will generate, through you, a more just
society and a better world.
God bless you, and may the joy of Jesus be always
with you.
Amen.

—JOHN PAUL II

Now, go in peace . . .
to love and serve the Lord.

John Paul II: A Biographical Sketch

Born on May 18, 1920, in Wadowice, Poland, Karol Józef Wojtyła was the third child of Karol Wojtyła and Emilia Kaczorowska. His mother died in 1929, the year he made his first Holy Communion, and his father died twelve years later.

Karol Wojtyła embarked on a promising academic career in 1938, when he enrolled in Jagiellonian University, in Kraków, and in a school for the dramatic arts. A year later, when the Nazi occupation forces closed the university, he was forced to leave school and go to work—first in a quarry and then in a chemical factory—to earn a living and avoid being deported to Germany.

During this time away from his studies, Wojtyła became aware of a call to the priesthood. In 1942, he began taking courses in the clandestine seminary of Kraków, run by Archbishop Adam Stefan Sapieha. At the same time, Wojtyła remained active in the theater, helping pioneer the underground Rhapsodic Theatre, a cultural resistance group.

When the Jagiellonian University reopened after the Second World War, Wojtyła resumed his studies in theology. He continued his courses for the priesthood at the major seminary in Kraków and was ordained on November 1, 1946.

Shortly after his ordination, Cardinal Sapieha sent Wojtyła to the Pontifical University of St. Thomas Aquinas, in Rome, for graduate studies. He completed his doctorate in theology in 1948 with a thesis on the problem of faith in the works of St. John of the Cross. During his vacations, he did pastoral work among the Polish immigrants of France, Belgium, and Holland.

Upon completing his doctorate, he returned to Poland, where he was vicar of various parishes in Kraków and chaplain for the university students. He returned to his studies on philosophy and theology in 1951, defending a second thesis in 1953 at the Catholic University of Lublin. A few years later, he joined the faculty of theology at Lublin and also became a professor of moral theology and social ethics in Kraków's major seminary.

On July 4, 1958, Pope Pius XII appointed Wojtyła auxiliary bishop of Kraków, and he was consecrated on September 28, 1958, in the city's Wawel Cathedral. Six years later, on January 13, 1964, he was nominated archbishop of Kraków by Pope Paul VI, who made him a cardinal on June 26, 1967.

As auxiliary bishop and then archbishop, Wojtyła took part in Vatican Council II, making an important contribution to the constitution *Gaudium et Spes*. As cardinal, he participated in all the assemblies of the Synod of Bishops.

On October 16, 1978, at the age of fifty-eight, Wojtyła was elected to the papacy, taking on the name John Paul II.

Over the course of his pontificate, Pope John Paul II traveled extensively. He completed 104 pastoral visits outside of Italy and 146 within Italy. As Bishop of Rome, he visited 317 of the city's 333 parishes.

In beatifying and canonizing more servants of God than any pope before him, John Paul II promoted the essential holiness of the Church, reaffirmed at Vatican II. He presided at 147 beatification ceremonies (1,338 blesseds proclaimed) and 51 canonization ceremonies (482 saints) during his pontificate. He held nine consistories, in which he created 231 cardinals.

No other pope encountered as many individuals as John Paul II did. More than 17 million pilgrims participated in his general audiences on Wednesdays. Millions more attended all the other special audiences and religious ceremonies held, including the more than 8 million pilgrims who traveled to Rome during the Great Jubilee of the Year 2000. In addition, there were the millions of faithful he met during pastoral visits in Italy and throughout the world, as well as the numerous government personalities he encountered during 38 official visits, 738 audiences and meetings with heads of state, and 246 audiences and meetings with prime ministers.

During the last years of his life, John Paul II battled Parkinson's disease and other illnesses, which limited his ability to travel and speak. He died on April 2, 2005, and his funeral drew millions of pilgrims to Rome, with millions more watching on televisions around the world.

The following are some notable dates in the pontificate of John Paul II:

JUNE 1979	Makes first pilgrimage to Poland
SEPTEMBER 1979	Begins four years of addresses on the "theology of the body"
OCTOBER 1979	Makes first pilgrimage to the United States
AUGUST 1980	Supports Solidarity trade union movement in Poland
MAY 13, 1981	Is shot in St. Peter's Square

DECEMBER 1983   Visits would-be assassin Mehmet Ali Acga in prison

JUNE 1985   Declares the Catholic commitment to ecumenism "irrevocable"

OCTOBER 1986   Invites world religious leaders for a day of prayer in Assisi

FALL 1989   Communist governments in Eastern Europe collapse

OCTOBER 1992   Corrects Church's handling of the Galileo case

DECEMBER 1992   Promulgates the *Catechism of the Catholic Church*

OCTOBER 1994   Publishes *Crossing the Threshold of Hope*

OCTOBER 1995   Addresses the United Nations in New York

MARCH 1998   Document *We Remember* reaches out to Jewish people

MARCH 2000   Issues formal apology for misdeeds of the Church over the centuries

AUGUST 2000   Attends Fifteenth World Youth Day, in Rome

MAY 2001   Becomes first pope to visit Greece since the Schism

OCTOBER 2002   Introduces the luminous mysteries and proclaims a Year of the Rosary

OCTOBER 2003	Celebrates twenty-fifth anniversary of his papacy
APRIL 2005	Dies at the age of eighty-four
JUNE 2005	Cause for sainthood is opened

Scripture and Other Quotations

CHAPTER 1

"Lord, teach us to pray." Luke 11:1

"Pray always without becoming weary." ["Then Jesus told them a parable about their need to pray always and not to lose heart." Luke 18:1]

"Helps us in our weakness" and "For we do not know how to pray as we ought, but that very Spirit intercedes with sighs too deep for words." Romans 8:26

"God, who searches the heart, knows what is the mind of the Spirit, because the Spirit intercedes for the saints according to the will of God." Romans 8:27

"Our Father who art in heaven" and "teach us to pray." ["He was praying in a certain place, and after he had finished, one of his disciples said to him, 'Lord, teach us to pray, as John taught his disciples.' He said to them, 'When you pray, say:

Father, hallowed by your name.
Your kingdom come.
Give us each day our daily bread.
And forgive us our sins, for we ourselves forgive everyone indebted to us.
And do not bring us to the time of trial.'"]
Luke 11:1–4

"Apart from me you can do nothing." John 15:5

"To the ends of the earth." Acts 13:47

CHAPTER 2

"But the tax collector, standing far off, would not even look up to heaven, but was beating his breast and saying, 'God, be merciful to me, a sinner!' I tell you, this man went down to his home justified rather than the other; for all who exalt themselves will be humbled, but all who humble themselves will be exalted." Luke 18:13–14

"Forgive us our trespasses, as we forgive those who trespass against us." ["And forgive us our debts, as we also have forgiven our debtors."] Matthew 6:12

"So my heavenly Father will also do to every one of you, if you do not forgive your brother or sister from your heart." Matthew 18:35

"Something against us." ["So when you are offering your gift at the altar, if you remember that your brother or sister has something against you, leave your gift there before the altar and go; first be reconciled to your brother or sister and then come and offer your gift."] Matthew 6:23–24

CHAPTER 3

"No one has ever seen God. It is God the only Son, who is close to the Father's heart, who has made him known." John 1:18

"You will know the truth, and the truth will make you free." John 8:32

"I am the life." ["I am the resurrection and the life."] John 11:25

"I came that they may have life." John 10:10

"I am the way, and the truth, and the life." John 14:6

"Go out into the roads and lanes." Luke 14:23

"Beware that no one leads you astray. For many will come in my name, saying, 'I am the Messiah!'" Matthew 24:4–5

"My time is near." Matthew 4:17

CHAPTER 4

"Whom God has given to those who obey him." Acts 5:32

"We must obey God rather than any human authority." Acts 5:29

"Increase our faith!" Luke 17:5

"Christ Jesus has made . . . his own." Philippians 3:12

"To the ends of the earth." Acts 13:47

"Now by this we may be sure that we know him, if we obey his commandments." 1 John 2:3

"You are the light of the world. . . . [L]et your light shine before others, so that they may see your good works and give glory to your Father in heaven." Matthew 5:14, 16

"Pray without ceasing." 1 Thessalonians 5:17

CHAPTER 5

"I was a stranger and you welcomed me." Matthew 25:35

"Ever since the creation of the world his eternal power and divine nature, invisible though they are, have been understood and seen through the things he has made." Romans 1:20

CHAPTER 6

"The eye is the lamp of the body. So, if your eye is healthy, your whole body will be full of light; but if your eye is unhealthy, your whole body will be full of darkness. If then the light in you is darkness, how great is the darkness!" Matthew 6:22–23

"I am the light of the world. Whoever follows me will never walk in darkness but will have the light of life." John 8:12

"Man's most secret core and his sanctuary [w]here he is alone with God." *Catechism of the Catholic Church* (section 1776)

"God, be merciful to me, a sinner!" Luke 18:13

CHAPTER 7

"It is to your advantage that I go away, for if I do not go away, the Advocate will not come to you; but if I go, I will send him to you." John 16:7

"I will not leave you orphaned; I am coming to you." John 14:18

"And remember, I am with you always, to the end of the age." Matthew 28:20

"The family of God, a fellowship afire with a unifying spirit." *Christifideles Laici* (26)

"Woe to me if I do not proclaim the gospel!" 1 Corinthians 9:16

"I am with you always." Matthew 28:20

"For nothing will be impossible with God." Luke 1:37

"Father's only son, full of grace and truth." John 1:14

"To purify and renew themselves so that the sign of Christ can shine more brightly on her face." *Lumen Gentium* (15)

"All the nations shall stream to it." Isaiah 2:2

CHAPTER 8

"Because there is one bread, we who are many are one body, for we all partake of the one bread." 1 Corinthians 10:17

"Peace be with you." Rite of Peace ["Peace to all of you who are in Christ." 1 Peter 5:14]

"Remember the church throughout the world." Eucharistic Prayer

"A new creation." 2 Corinthians 5:17

"I am with you always, to the end of the age." Matthew 28:20

"The dispersed children of God." John 11:52

"My Father is still working, and I also am working." John 5:17

"In spirit and truth." John 4:23

"By this everyone will know that you are my disciples, if you have love for one another." John 13:35

CHAPTER 9

"Unless you change and become like children, you will never enter the kingdom of heaven." Matthew 18:3

"That they may all be one. As you, Father, are in me and I am in you, may they also be in us." John 17:21

"This is a great mystery." Ephesians 5:32

"Husbands, love your wives, just as Christ loved the church and gave himself up for her." Ephesians 5:25

"Therefore what God has joined together, let no one separate." Matthew 19:6; Mark 10:9

"In the image of God." Genesis 1:27

"Therefore what God has joined together, let no one separate." Matthew 19:6; Mark 10:9

"The fruit of the spirit is love, joy, peace, patience, kindness, generosity, faithfulness, gentleness, and self-control." Galatians 5:22–23

"Man is more precious for what he is than for what he has." *Gaudium et Spes*, part 1, chapter 3, section 35

"It is not good that the man should be alone; I will make him a helper as his partner." Genesis 2:18

"In old age they still produce fruit; they are always green and full of sap, showing that the Lord is upright." Psalm 92:14–15

CHAPTER 10

"Just as you did it to one of the least of these who are members of my family, you did it to me." Matthew 25:40

"Loved us and gave himself up for us." Ephesians 5:2

"Very truly, I tell you, you will weep and mourn, but the world will rejoice." John 16:20

"You will have pain, but your pain will turn into joy." John 16:20

"Blessed are those who mourn, for they will be comforted. Blessed are those who are persecuted for righteousness' sake, for theirs is the kingdom of heaven. Blessed are you when people revile you and persecute you and utter all kinds of evil against you falsely on my account. Rejoice and be glad, for your reward is great in heaven." Matthew 5:4, 10–12

"Yet, not my will but yours be done." Luke 22:42 (Matthew 26:39; Mark 14:36)

"Very truly, I tell you, unless a grain of wheat falls into the earth and dies, it remains just a single grain; but if it dies, it bears much fruit." John 12:24

"So death is at work in us, but life in you." 2 Corinthians 4:12

"I am filled with consolation; I am overjoyed in all our affliction." 2 Corinthians 7:4

"Am I my brother's keeper?" Genesis 4:9

"What have you done? Listen; your brother's blood is crying out to me from the ground!" Genesis 4:10

"The Son of Man has nowhere to lay his head." Matthew 8:20; Luke 9:58

"But our citizenship is in heaven." Philippians 3:20

"Do not store up for yourselves treasures on earth, where moth and rust consume and where thieves break in and steal; but store up for yourselves treasures in heaven." Matthew 6:19–20

"But she out of her poverty has put in everything she had, all she had to live on." Mark 12:44

"If I give away all my possessions, . . . but do not have love, I gain nothing." 1 Corinthians 13:3

CHAPTER 11

"Calls his own sheep by name." John 10:3

"Do whatever he tells you." John 2:5

"And God saw that it was good." Genesis 1:4, 12, 18, 21, 24, 31

"Where did this man get all this? What is this wisdom that has been given to him? What deeds of power are being done by his hands! Is not this the carpenter?" Mark 6:2–3

"Cursed is the ground because of you; in toil you shall eat of it all the days of your life." Genesis 3:17

"New heavens and a new earth." 2 Peter 3:13

CHAPTER 12

"Blessed be the God and Father of our Lord Jesus Christ, who has blessed us in Christ with every spiritual blessing in the heavenly places, just as he chose us in Christ before the foundation of the world to be holy and blameless before him in love." Ephesians 1:3–4

"Rich in mercy." Ephesians 2:4

"Sees in secret." Matthew 6:18

"Dwells in unapproachable light." 1 Timothy 6:16

"Ever since the creation of the world his eternal power and divine nature, invisible though they are, have been understood and seen through the things he has made." Romans 1:20

"No one has ever seen God." John 1:18; 1 John 4:12

"The only Son, who is close to the Father's heart, who has made him known." John 1:18

"Keep the commandments." Matthew 19:17

"This is my commandment, that you love one another as I have loved you." John 15:12

"So if I, your Lord and Teacher, have washed your feet, you also ought to wash one another's feet. For I have set you an example, that you also should do as I have done to you." John 13:14–15

"I give you a new commandment, that you love one another. Just as I have loved you, you also should love one another. By this everyone will know that you are my disciples, if you have love for one another." John 13:34–35

"As the Father has loved me, so I have loved you; abide in my love." John 15:9

"God's love has been poured into our hearts through the Holy Spirit that has been given to us." Romans 5:5

"The law indeed was given through Moses; grace and truth came through Jesus Christ." John 1:17

"For your own lifeblood I will surely require a reckoning: . . . each one for the blood of another, I will require a reckoning for human life." Genesis 9:5

"So God created humankind in his image." Genesis 1:27

"In his hand is the life of every living thing and the breath of every human being." Job 12:10

"The Lord kills and brings to life; he brings down to Sheol and raises up." 1 Samuel 2:6

"It is I who bring both death and life." ["I have set before you life and death." Deuteronomy 30:19; "I am setting before you the way of life and the way of death." Jeremiah 21:8]

"Prince of Peace." Isaiah 9:6

"Peace I leave with you; my peace I give to you." John 14:27

"You shall love your neighbor as yourself." Mark 12:31

Sources

"Learning to Pray," September 1, 1980

Familiaris Consortio, November 22, 1981, nn. 59, 60

Reconciliatio et Paenitentia, 1984, n. 12

Dominum et Vivicantem, May 18, 1986, nn. 12, 65

Address at Williams-Brice Stadium, Columbia, SC, September 11, 1987

"Prayer Must Be United to Action," May 5, 1988

Christifidelis Laici, December 30, 1988, nn. 18, 29, 30

Message for the Twenty-fifth World Day of Prayer for Peace, January 1, 1992

Address to the First World Congress for pilgrimage leaders and directors of pilgrimage shrines, February 28, 1992

General audience on the Holy Eucharist in the life of the Church, April 8, 1992

General audience on the Sacrament of Penance, April 15, 1992

Catechesis on prayer during a general audience, September 9, 1992

Message to the world's leaders and all people of goodwill on a particular aspect of peace, December 8, 1992

Ad limina address to the bishops of Alabama, Kentucky, Louisiana, Mississippi, and Tennessee, June 5, 1993

Letter to the bishops of the United States on the recent scandal given by members of the clergy, June 11, 1993

Speech at Stapleton International Airport, Denver, CO, August 12, 1993

Address to the Eighth World Youth Day, Denver, CO, August 14, 1993

Homily at Sunday Mass on World Youth Day, Cherry Creek State Park, Denver, CO, August 15, 1993

Ad limina address to the bishops of New England, September 21, 1993

Letter to President Clinton, released April 5, 1994, by the U.S. Embassy to the Vatican

Christmas message to children, December 13, 1994

Urbi et Orbi, Christmas message, December 25, 1994

Evangelium Vitae, March 25, 1995, n. 83

L'Osservatore Romano, English edition, May 5, 1995

Message on the Fourth U.N. Conference on Women, May 26, 1995

Address to associations belonging to the Italian Federation of Therapeutic Communities, June 26, 1995

"All Must Strive for Goal of Full Unity," 132nd address on the mystery of the Church, July 12, 1995

Address for World Migration Day, July 25, 1995

"Di fronte alle," 137th address on the mystery of the Church, August 30, 1995

"Give Them Something to Eat," message for Lent 1996, September 8, 1995

Address to the U.N. General Assembly, October 5, 1995

Homily at a Mass at Aqueduct Racetrack, Queens, NY, October 6, 1995

Homily at a Mass in Central Park, NY, October 7, 1995

Homily at a Mass at Oriole Park at Camden Yards, Baltimore, MD, October 8, 1995

Address to the Pontifical Commission for the Cultural Heritage of the Church, October 12, 1995

Address at the Twenty-eighth Conference of the U.N. Food and Agriculture Organization, October 23, 1995

Address to the Pontifical Academy for Life, November 20, 1995

Address to the Congregation for the Doctrine of the Faith at the conclusion of their plenary session, November 24, 1995

Message for the Eleventh World Youth Day in 1996, November 26, 1995

Message for the 1996 World Day of Peace, December 8, 1995

"En Esta Occasion," message to the Church in Cuba, February 2, 1996

Address to Cardinal William W. Baum and the Apostolic Penitentiary, March 22, 1996

Message for World Mission Sunday, May 28, 1996

Address on the U.N. Conference on Human Settlements, June 16, 1996

Address at an ecumenical Liturgy of the Word with representatives of non-Catholic churches in Germany, June 22, 1996

"The Season of Lent," message for Lent 1997, October 25, 1996

Message for the World Day of Prayer for Vocations, October 28, 1996

Address to the World Food Summit, November 13, 1996

Address to a joint session of all the Pontifical Academies, November 28, 1996

Address at a conference sponsored by the Pontifical Council for Pastoral Assistance to Health-Care Workers, November 30, 1996

"Motherhood, Woman's Gift to Society," address to an international meeting promoting the well-being of women, December 7, 1996

Address on the World Day of Peace, December 8, 1996

Prayer for the First Year of the Immediate Preparation for the Great Jubilee Year 2000, January 14, 1997

Message for the Thirty-first World Communications Day, January 24, 1997

Ad limina address to the bishops of France, January 25, 1997

Catechesis on the dignity of human work, March 19, 1997

Address to the youth of Rome, St. Peter's Square, March 20, 1997

"The Environment and Health," address to a convention, March 24, 1997

Address to the pontifical council "Cor Unum," April 18, 1997

Address to the Pontifical Academy of Social Sciences, April 25, 1997

Message for World Mission Sunday, May 18, 1997

Address at an ecumenical prayer service in Poland, May 31, 1997

Address to the World Congress of Gynecological Endoscopy, June 21, 1997

Second World Meeting with Families, Rio de Janeiro, October 5, 1997

Christmas Eve homily, midnight Mass, December 24, 1997

Urbi et Orbi, Easter Sunday, April 12, 1998

Dies Domini, Pentecost Sunday, May 31, 1998

Fides et Ratio, September 18, 1998, greeting, 12, 13, 16, 18, 27, 31, 32, 92

Incarnationis Mysterium, Bull of Indictment of the Great Jubilee of the Year 2000, November 29, 1998